MW01631870

DON'T F*CKING SAY THAT

A GUIDE FOR AVOIDING WELL-INTENTIONED WORDS THAT MAKE TOUGH TIMES TOUGHER

MELLISSA LIBRACH

DON'T F*CKING SAY THAT
A Guide for Avoiding Well-Intentioned Words
that Make Tough Times Tougher
First Edition

ISBN 978-1-962341-42-4 *Hardcover*
978-1-962341-41-7 *Paperback*
978-1-962341-43-1 *Ebook*
978-1-962341-44-8 *Audiobook*

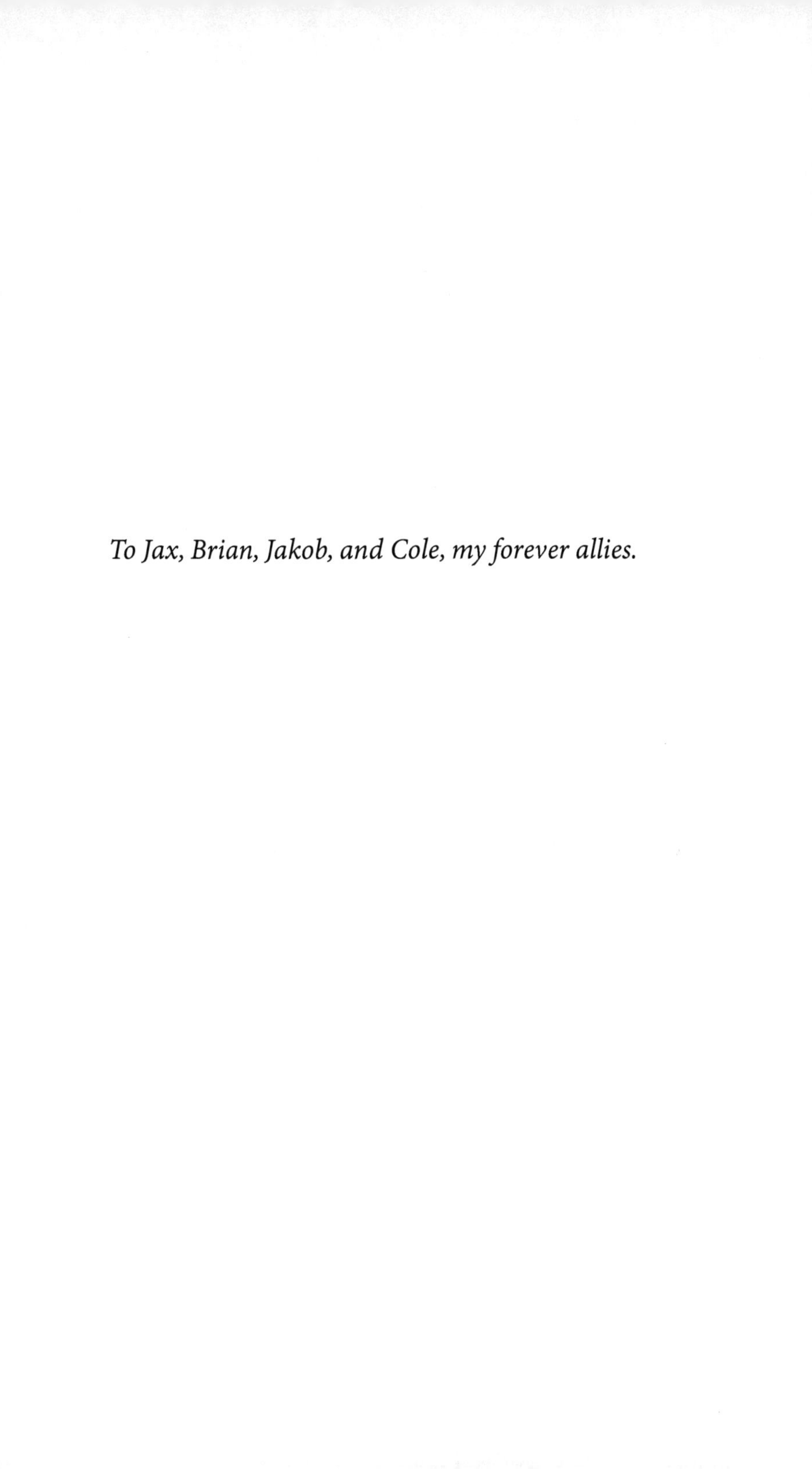

To Jax, Brian, Jakob, and Cole, my forever allies.

C*NTENTS

THE **IMPACT** YOU HAVE ON OTHERS IS MORE IMPORTANT THAN YOUR **INTENTION.**

INTRODUCTION

"That's why understanding the difference between intent and impact is critical: It can quite literally be the difference between suffering and love."

—Vienna Pharaon

"At least you got a boob job out of the deal!"

In case your jaw didn't immediately drop when you read the above comment, let me just gently make something very clear:

That's *not* something you should ever say to a breast cancer survivor who's just had a mastectomy.

How do I know? Because someone said that to me. Recently.

And if your jaw *did* just drop in shock, then boy do I have news for you: that's not even the tip of the iceberg of what you'll read in this book! Pop some popcorn and settle in, because you're about to cringe your ass off. (But the fun kind of cringe. Like watching *The Office.*)

Yes, in the year of our lord 2023, as I was heading in for another surgery in my fight against breast cancer, someone actually offered the "silver lining" that at least I was getting a boob job.

Hmmmm... not exactly what's top of mind right now, but thanks.

Now, I know what you're probably thinking.

They meant well.

They were just trying to make you feel better.

They had the best of intentions.

You know what? I agree with you on all points. Nobody's walking around in the world saying to themselves, "Hey, what's something I can say that will absolutely *ruin* the day of someone going through a bad time?" Everyone has the best of intentions, and most people genuinely want to be helpful and supportive when the people in their lives need comfort.

But here's the problem: those well-intentioned words so often have the opposite effect. And no matter what someone's intention is, the impact of their words can be a punch in the gut.

Or a knife, twisting into your gut up to the handle.

Either one.

Sounds dramatic, I know, but if you've ever been on the receiving end of one of the classics during a time of personal crisis or tragedy—an "At least...", maybe, or a "Have you tried..."—then I would bet anything you're nodding your head in recognition.

Going through tragedy *sucks*. Going through it while hearing platitudes that make you want to smack someone upside the head is even worse.

Going through all that while tiptoeing around trying not to make anyone feel bad... now that's where things get *really* fun!

You're about to journey through a whole jungle of well-intentioned words that were said to me as I traversed tough times in my life—of which I've had maybe a little more than my fair share, but hey, as Eckhart Tolle says, *it is as it is.*

Through each story, my hope is that you'll get a sense of why sometimes the common comfort people offer up in times of crisis actually hurts worse than saying nothing at all. You'll also see examples of what you *can* say. Words that actually lift and inspire, offer hope, or even just send the message that you care and you're there for them.

I'm offering up my story as a guidebook of sorts, to help you gain a better understanding of how to offer *real* support, the kind that will truly help someone going through a tough time.

DON'T MAKE ANYBODY FEEL BAD

When I think back on the "boob job" moment, as I call it, I like to imagine that I turned on that person with the perfect mix of righteous anger and patient teaching, showed them the error of their ways, and walked away knowing I'd saved a future fellow cancer fighter from such a banger of a comment.

But I didn't.

My reaction wasn't to fire back, get mad, tell the person off, or really to say anything at all.

My reaction was to smile tightly and quickly turn away so the words that wanted to claw their way out of my throat didn't come flying at the person like a dozen hand grenades.

I *wanted* to tell them that they had no idea what they were talking about. That they should probably keep their mouth shut. That, *great*, now I would need to take time out of my day to go sit in my car and breathe for a few minutes to get over the piercing flash of pain, embarrassment, anger, and grief that had shot through me like lightning at their words.

That's often what it feels like to be on the receiving end of comments like that. It feels like a whiplash of hurt that we're just expected to smile through.

Smile, don't react, and *definitely* don't say what we're thinking.

Because if we respond with what we're really feeling, or even a polite, "Hey, that actually kind of hurts, maybe don't say things like that," then we've made the person feel bad.

And if there's anything people having tough times are *not* supposed to do, it's make *other* people feel bad, right?

It's absolutely crazy, but anyone who's been in my shoes knows it's the truth. The number one priority in our society is not to offend someone else, even if they've said something absolutely batshit crazy to you.

So much so that I wrestled for a long time with the decision to write this book. I thought to myself, *am I being ungrateful? Am I being too hard on people who have the best of intentions?*

Then I read a quote that stuck with me:

The impact you have on others is more important than your intention.

Think about that.

Think back to every time someone said something that hurt you, and then followed it up by insisting, "But I meant well."

"I didn't *mean* to stick this knife in your guts and twist hard! I was just trying to help!" Oh, okay, never mind then! I'll go find a band-aid and shut up.

Imagine if instead, they just apologized for the impact they made, and tried to do better in the future.

Just imagine how much better off we'd all be if focused

more on our impact than our intention. If we stopped using our intentions as a get out of jail free card for hurting people.

In the moments when I've heard a comment that cut me to the bone—no matter what the person's intent was—I had two options.

Option A: what I described earlier, which basically amounts to smiling through gritted teeth, excusing myself, and going out to my car for some deep breathing.

Option B: Try to teach that person how not to hurt someone else the way they just hurt me.

That second option became my preferred option after a while. I'm not sure if it took me that long to build up the courage, or if I just got my buttons pushed one too many times... but eventually, I found that I actually had comebacks at the ready.

Like, "Oh yeah, I sent my surgeon a card thanking him for the boob job... and for saving my life."

Or, "Totally! That's exactly what I was thinking while puking my guts out after my third round of chemo!"

Snarky? Hell yes. But I managed to add in just enough humor and compassion that I could turn those comebacks into teachable moments. It felt like a side quest in the larger battle against cancer: spare the next person by cutting the "well-intentioned" comments off at the source.

The comebacks helped me get some of the power back that had been wrenched away by the disease. Every time I got hit with a "well-intentioned" comment, I reframed my mindset. I'm not going to get upset, because I have the courage and ability to teach you not to say it again.

But—look. I'll just be blunt.

I'm tired of teaching.

After a while, teachable moments get exhausting.

The people in your life who have to keep teaching you how not to hurt them are tired. I'm tired. I have cancer. I don't have time to teach you how to be. That's why I wrote this book.

I believe beyond a shadow of a doubt that most people are just good people trying to get along. That pretty much everyone has the best of intentions and truly does not want to cause harm.

In fact, you can rest easy knowing that I assume you're a good person trying not to hurt people.

The problem is... sometimes, you might.

And you know what?

That's okay.

It doesn't make you a bad person. It just makes you someone who needs to learn how to say the right thing (and how to definitely avoid saying the wrong thing).

Luckily, you now have this book in your hands. You're holding the bible on what not to say to someone having a tough time. Take your foot all the way out of your mouth, because once you're done reading, it's never going back in again!

A UNIVERSAL EXPERIENCE

Right after I was diagnosed with cancer at age 44, my little sister got her diagnosis as well at age 40.

It's not funny. It's not. But did we laugh at the sheer ridiculousness of it? Yeah, a little bit. Like, who exactly did we piss off up there?

Taking that energy with her into the journey of fighting cancer ended up being a good thing. She would need that laughter as a reaction when she started getting the "well intentioned comments" I knew would be coming her way. The fact that I had already lived through some tragedies and had been hearing "cancer platitudes" for months turned out to have one perk: I was able to be my sister's guide, of sorts, through the confusing, jaw-dropping maze of those comments.

She'd call me up and say, "Listen to what someone said today..." and we'd just laugh. I kept telling her to hold on to that hilarity. Keep seeing it as the absolutely ridiculous bullshit it was. That was the only way she would stay sane.

We had to laugh, or we would cry. Pro tragedy tip: always inject laughter. It's how we move on and not hold it against people—unless they're repeat offenders, in which case your only good options are "set them straight" or "avoid forever".

But it did get to her. A few weeks in, she called me up and was yelling even before the call had fully connected.

All I heard was, "—SWEAR TO GOD IF ONE MORE PERSON SAYS I GOT THE GOOD KIND OF CANCER—"

"What?" I said. "Someone said that?"

"They're *all* saying that," she told me. "What exactly is *the good cancer?!* It's *cancer!* There's no *good!"*

Other choice nuggets she heard:

"You'll be okay, you'll make it through, because you're

strong." *So everyone who lost their battle with cancer was a weak little bitch, I guess?*

"At least you got an easier surgery..." *Have you ever had your lymph nodes removed? How about I take an ice cream scoop to your armpit?*

"Are you going to get a double mastectomy?" *Since when is it socially acceptable to walk around asking people what body parts they're removing?*

"Oh, I knew someone with that cancer... they died." *GREAT, LOVE TO HEAR IT, THANKS.*

She'd call me up weekly for reassurance that she wasn't crazy for feeling crazy. I was able to validate the hell out of her experience, because—sadly—it's a universal one. The thing no one prepares you for when tragedy strikes is all the out-of-touch, tactless nonsense people are going to hurl your way.

Even though I'd been through a lot of the same words, hearing my sister's experience *still* always shocked me. It shocked me to hear what people were saying. And that's good—because what my sister desperately needed to feel was validation. We're told not to take it personally, that "people mean well" and "people are doing their best".

I knew she needed to hear, "You're not crazy. That is a fucked up thing to say."

It can really get under your skin. It can make you start to question your own reality. Once, she was accused of "using cancer to her benefit so she could stay home from work as much as she wanted." (Yeah. You read that right.)

Her mind was so twisted around from everything people had been throwing at her that she actually started questioning if she *was* using cancer as an excuse to stay home from work. "*Am* I lazy?" she asked me. "Am I being a baby for staying in bed after chemo?"

These "well-intentioned" comments prey on every last insecurity you have. That's a big reason why they hurt so much.

When people are going through tough times, here's what they need:

Authenticity.

The real you. Even if you're awkward. Even if you're unsure what to say.

Truth.

"Fuck. This sucks. I love you. You're not alone. I'm here."

It seems like it's too little, like it's not saying anything profound—but simple, authentic, truthful statements like that are actually *monumental* to someone going through it. Because at that moment, when they're scared, sad, angry, grieving, or all of the above, hearing that they're loved and they're not alone is the best medicine they could hope for.

A worthless platitude about everything happening for a reason... get out of here with that.

IT'S NOT ABOUT YOU

If you're struggling a little with the whole intention vs. impact thing, and you're a little stuck on feeling hurt that your good intentions are being deprioritized for the hurt feelings of people experiencing tragedy, listen up:

It's not about you.

One of the funniest and most telling things that has been happening to me lately is friends who know I'm writing this book coming up to me saying, "Just tell me which chapter is mine. I know I'm probably all over the place in the book. Just tell me where I can find myself so I can read it and prepare."

My best friend—spoiler alert—knew *exactly* which chapter would be hers before I even started writing. "Mell, you might as well just title the 'silver lining' chapter with my name. That's okay, bring it on, I can take it."

Here's the thing.

It's not about you. I promise.

I didn't write this book in response to any one person, and this book isn't about anyone but *me.* My feelings, my experiences, and my thoughts on how we can all support each other better.

At the end of the day, that's what we all want to do, right? We want to show the people we love that we love them. Humans are naturally empathetic beings, despite what the news and social media makes things look like (and I'll talk more about this later, but I don't watch the news, and I don't do social media for that exact reason). We *want* to love each other. We want to support each other. When another person is in pain, our natural instinct and urge is to reach out and help, even if the only thing we have to offer is comfort.

That's why I wrote this book. I wanted to create a message of love for everyone who has ever tried to support someone who's hurting, and accidentally made things worse.

I wanted to say: "I see you. I know you're trying your best. I know you don't know what to say. I know you only want to help."

I wanted to add my own help to the mix, giving you the tools you need to carry out your original mission—to love and support the person you care about.

I also wanted to send a message of solidarity to everyone who's experienced tragedy and gone through those lightning-bolt, whiplash, *did you really just say that?!* moments. I see you, too. I know it's hard to hear those words, and I know it's even harder not to react, get mad, and make anyone else feel bad. I know all too well what it feels like to walk on eggshells trying not to upset anyone when *you're* the one who's going through it.

I had already been through two major once-in-a-lifetime tragedies by the time I was diagnosed with cancer. I'd already been through the "well-intentioned" wringer. Through the haze of getting handed a cancer diagnosis, a big part of me was thinking, *god dammit. Here we go again.* I knew exactly what I was in for.

It's exhausting. It makes you want to crawl into bed, pull your covers over your head, and never ever come out and see anyone, ever again. I know how lonely it feels when nobody else gets it. I know how isolating grief is. *I see you.*

My hope for *you* is that you see yourself in these pages and know that you're not alone. And maybe that you get some much-needed laughter, which I truly believe is one of the best medicines there is.

If you're anything like my friends and family who I've shared these "well-intentioned" comments with over the years, then you might find some of them unbelievable—and funny. *So* funny. You'll probably laugh your ass off, actually, and then wonder if you're allowed to laugh at this stuff.

I promise—you are! Please laugh. Yes, some of what you'll read is dark, but if you ask me, sometimes dark humor is the best humor. Anyone who's been through trauma knows that when you go through shit, your sense of humor gets WILD. There's a lot of my dark humor in these stories. Go ahead: laugh, wince, cry, and have all the reactions that bubble up as you make your way through these pages.

This book is, above all else, optimistic. I really believe we all want to have the best impact we can. I'm sharing this without any anger or bitterness—only love, a little bit of humor, and in the hope that we can all support each other even better.

And if you're afraid of getting your feelings hurt, you *really* need to read this book. (Plus, if your fear of being told you messed up outweighs your fear of hurting someone... your priorities need to be examined. Period.)

So swallow your pride, read this book cover to cover, and then go hug someone you love.

And, for the love of God... *don't fucking say that!*

EMOTIONS ARE **ROUGH.** TRAGEDY IS **ROUGH.** IT'S HARD ENOUGH WHEN WE HAVE **OUR OWN EMOTIONS** TO BE THERE FOR, LET ALONE **SOMEONE ELSE'S.**

CH*PTER ONE

AT LEAST...

Let's kick off this party with what is probably the most commonly used "well-intentioned" phrase of all: the "at least" opener.

Picture this:

You're in a dark well of emotion due to shit going down in your life. Maybe someone died; maybe you're battling a health issue; maybe you've just been handed divorce papers. Whatever it is, your life has blown up, and you've been totally decimated by the shrapnel.

But today, you've actually managed to do what's felt impossible for days/weeks: you've pulled yourself out of bed and actually gone out into the world. Sure, it's only because there's no food in the house, and despite not having the emotional energy to care about being hungry, your body is demanding a meal—and your bank account can only sustain so many Uber Eats hits. So here you are, weakly pushing a shopping cart down the frozen food aisle at your local Publix.

You're staring at the rows and rows of packaged food behind the frosty glass of the freezer doors, trying to muster the energy to grab a lasagna or a bag of broccoli. Suddenly, you hear your name called from somewhere behind you. Oh no. Not now.

You turn around, dreading the human contact... and sure enough, there's a fellow mom from your kid's playgroup barreling down the aisle at you. It's the first time she's seen you since it all happened. She has that look in her eye, like she's been waiting for the opportunity to offer "support". It's not that you don't appreciate the thought, but you know what's coming. This isn't your first tragedy rodeo. You brace yourself.

You know the "at least" grenade is about to be lobbed directly at your head.

What exactly does it sound like? Well, here's a personal example:

"At least you can still have kids."

That was something I heard a lot after I lost my first son, Jacob, at 23 weeks.

If you're thinking, no WAY would someone say something that insensitive to a grieving mother, then boy, you should really strap in for the rest of this book!

Also, think back to every conversation you've ever been either in or near with someone who's going through tragedy. Think hard.

You've definitely heard the "at least" opener.

It's like a reflex when people find themselves talking to someone they know who's having a tough time. "At least they didn't suffer." "At least you got to say goodbye." "At least your prognosis is good." "At least you still have your other kid(s)."

Yeah, that last one is also something I've heard a lot when telling Jacob's story. Because after the brutal, life-shattering death of my first son, I did eventually go on to become the mother of my second son, Jax. It felt like feeling and optimism coming back into a numb world.

But I don't want to think of Jax as an "at least". And I don't consider his birth—as deliriously, indescribably happy as it made me and my husband, Brian—to be in any way a lessening of the pain of losing Jacob. One child's life doesn't erase the pain of another's death.

And honestly, I don't think anyone who's ever dropped an "at least" would disagree with that. Asked about it after the fact, someone who literally just told someone an "at least..." statement would likely say, "Oh, yeah, you should never say that." As though they themselves didn't just do so.

And yet we, the ones eating the shit sandwich that fate has so cruelly dealt us, keep hearing it.

So where does the "at least" opener come from? Why is it so prevalent? If basically everyone agrees it's a no-no, why does it come out like a reflex whenever someone encounters a tragedy-struck person in their life?

To answer that question, I think we should first dive into what's happening in the mind of the attempted support-giver, the one dropping those well-intentioned words and accidentally setting off a mental bonfire for the person they're trying to comfort.

MAIN CHARACTER SYNDROME

I promise I'm not being judgmental when I say this:

People tend to see the world through the lens of their own experience.

Is that another way of saying people tend to be self-centered? Yes. They are. You are, I am, we all are. (I'm literally sitting here writing a book about myself right now.)

That's normal. Being self-centered makes sense—our experience is the only one we have, so of course that's our default lens for seeing the world. And, sure, we have empathy, but it can only take us so far into someone else's viewpoint. Typically, when you're talking to someone, the default mode is to be thinking: How does what they're saying translate into my own experience, so I can understand and relate? In this way, our default self-centeredness is often a way we're trying to actually connect. We're looking for points of similarity, common experiences that will allow us to say, "I get it. I've been there. I see you."

At the end of the day, being seen and known by others is one of our primary drivers. We really, really want to be understood. It makes us feel safe, special, and validated. (See: all of social media. We go to bed feverishly checking how many likes we got on our most recent post, and we wake up and grab for our phones to see how many people liked us while we slept.)

So there's nothing wrong with being self-centered.

But there is something wrong with making yourself the main character in someone else's story.

I have a theory that many people out there are more interested in putting on the performance of support than actually being supportive.

What does true support require? It requires de-centering yourself. It requires shutting up, listening, and acting wholly in service of the person you're supporting, without the expectation of recognition. True support is living into the phrase, "It's not about me", and removing yourself as the main character—or, really, anything other than an extra—in the story for a while.

A lot of people can't handle this. They don't know how to do this. This may be the first time you're hearing this, and you might be uncomfortable, and that's okay. They're so accustomed to being the main character that they get twitchy whenever someone else has the spotlight. Even calling it that—the spotlight—makes me laugh, because who the hell wants the spotlight of tragedy glaring in their face? Nobody wants to be the main character in a sad story.

Well... except some people. You ever have one of those people in your life who everything seems to happen to, all the time? They're constantly having issues, other people are constantly mistreating them, they've always got something tragic looming in the background? The type of person that eventually leads you to say, "This many bad things do not happen to a single person...what's going on here?" What's going on is pretty simple: they've seen that experiencing tough times automatically turns you into the main character, and they want that attention so badly that they manufacture a life of constant turmoil to get it. If they're not inside the drama, they're not "important". They're not special. In their world, the amount of drama you're going through is directly proportional to how important you are.

The irony of going through real tragedy is that the last thing you want when you're grieving is attention. You don't want everyone looking at you, asking you how they can help. You're grateful for the attempted support, but managing everyone's attempts to be part of the story is exhausting.

Because that's what a lot of performative support looks like. It's not authentic; it's not coming from a place of real empathy.

It's a knee jerk reaction to suddenly not being the main character in the story.

This is the root of where the "at least..." opener, and most of the "well-intentioned words" in this book, come from.

The scene typically goes like this:

1. Taylor gets kicked in the ass by life. She's suddenly the main character of a shitty story she wouldn't wish on their worst enemy. Being the main character, all attention is on her.

2. Allison is suddenly out of the spotlight. (Remember, we're all walking around as the main character of our own story.) She's uncomfortable with this. She doesn't know how to handle being totally de-centered, something being completely not

about her in any way.

3. Allison sees Taylor in the frozen food aisle and instinctively tries to take back some of that spotlight. How do you get credit in a movie? You have lines. Allison blurts out some random script she heard somewhere, lines that she doesn't even deliver believably, words that allow her to put on the performance of support without actually doing it. "At least..."

4. Taylor inwardly flinches at the verbal nightmare being inflicted upon them; outwardly, she smiles and musters her own performance, saying the lines that will allow her to exit stage right and get out of the unwanted spotlight as quickly as possible. "I appreciate it" and "thanks, I'll let you know" and "I'm taking it one day at a time." Or she freezes and says nothing at all—and just a hint, if you've ever had someone freeze up in response to your well-intentioned words, inwardly they're dying a little. Sometimes you can't even muster a response.

5. Satisfied that she's played at least a supporting role

> in the story, Allison continues on with her grocery shopping. Taylor goes out to her car and [insert your preferred mental breakdown—anything from thousand-yard stare to dissolving into sobs].

Now, if you've only ever been the Allison in that scenario, you might be a little miffed. But I'm not trying to be the main character! I'm just trying to be supportive and make sure they know I'm there for them and offer them some comfort... I'm going to stop you right there. Notice the "I" statements? Notice how it's all about what you're doing, and not about what they're needing? Notice how you're still making the story about you?

I get it; I do. It's really, really hard to decenter ourselves in what's happening, but it's impossible to offer real support unless you do.

When someone comes along who offers true support—who understands that they're not the main character, that it's not about them, and doesn't expect credit, let alone anything in return—it's such an intense relief for Taylor.

Finally, here's someone I don't have to perform for.

"Crazy how quickly you learn what not to say when you enter the cancer arena. Especially when you're only in your 20s and you have lymphoma.

My mom and I have just tried to have a sense of humor now that we have had a little time to get used to saying the word.

Some of the best, funniest exchanges have happened to my mom. An acquaintance stopped her on the street, proceeded with the unwelcome litany of questions about what kind of cancer I have, treatment plans, stage, etc. And then she comforted my mom with, "I hear people can live a while with lymphoma". (My mom has since developed a stock response of "Thank you for your support" because saying "Fuck off, you idiot" wouldn't be super nice.)

People are happy to comfort me with "there are lots of ways to have a family", "you are actually so lucky it's lymphoma", "hair grows back" (sure, as long as it's not you that's bald), "you are the strongest person I know" (that one I get every day). "I have a neighbor, and his cousin's brother's roommate had cancer and he had 47 rounds of chemo..." Okay, how does that affect me exactly?

But anytime someone asks me the simple question that actually matters—"How are you doing?"—I just respond by singing "Stayin' Alive"..."

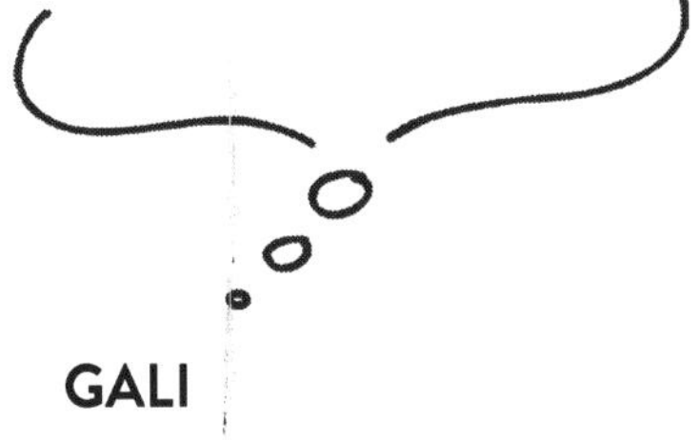

GALI

Here's someone who gets that this spotlight sucks and isn't trying to make me stand in it and say my lines so they can say their lines and get their credit.

Here's someone who's not going to word-vomit a "support" script at me that's going to send me into a grief spiral.

Here's someone who gets that the last thing I have energy for right now is ensuring they get to feel like part of the story.

It's funny; when truly supporting, you actually do become the star of the show, inadvertently. People remember you. They want to celebrate you. You do get the attention, just not in the way the people who actually want it care about. It's the people who aren't seeking the spotlight who end up getting it—and by being a true support, you enter as the understudy and exit as Best Supporting Actor.

True support means dropping the script entirely. Nobody has to say any lines, because there's no spotlight anymore.

CHAPTER ONE

TELL ME WHAT TO SAY

This is the first chapter, so this is where I'm going to set some ground rules.

First, I'm not going to tell you what to say instead of "at least..." or whatever other well-intentioned words we explore throughout the book.

Why, you ask? Well, it's pretty simple: if I give you a script, that means you're still performing.

And part of my intention with this book is to get you out of performance and into authenticity.

When I started talking to people in my life about some of the well-intentioned words I was hearing as I lost my son, the reactions were really split down the middle. People who had only ever been the Taylor character would immediately commiserate and share some of the batshit crazy stuff people had said to them. People who had only ever been Allison, though? They'd do one of two things.

One: try to defend the person who'd said the well-intentioned words to me, usually by defending the intention rather than understanding the impact. "They meant well... they don't know what to say... they just want to support." Okay, cool, but I had to take the grenade to the head, so what are we even talking about here? When people step up as white knights for other people's well-intentioned words, you know they're actually trying to defend themselves. And I don't have time for that. This isn't about you.

Two: say something like, "I get it, but it's hard to know what to say. What should they have said?" In other words: Give me a script so I don't fuck up like this in the future. Tell me what to say.

I'm not going to do that. First, while I'm sympathetic for the position you're in, it's not my responsibility to make sure you don't hurt someone's feelings; it's yours. And second, I don't want to give you a script to read. I want you to put the script down and actually be there for someone.

Why do we all cling to the script so hard?

I think I know why. It's because we're using it as a shield.

Emotions are rough. Tragedy is rough. It's hard enough when we have our own emotions to be there for, let alone someone else's.

When I lost Jacob, and the Person Bs in my world would find me in the supermarket and start reading the script—"How are you holding up?" "At least you're up and about already", etc.—I knew they expected me to read my pre-approved lines back to them. They were using the script as a shield.

They didn't want to hear the truth, because it was too painful, too uncomfortable. No one wants to be part of the story when it hurts that bad.

They didn't want to hear:

"How am I holding up? Well, I hate myself for not being able to hold onto my baby. I hate my body for losing him. I'm frozen in the moment when we buried him, like time left me there, paralyzed. Which, by the way, did you know that when you bury a baby that wasn't full-term, they walk you over to the bargain section of the cemetery and say, 'This is where people typically go when it's a miscarriage'? Like I didn't actually give birth to him. Like I didn't push him out of me. When he was about to be born, I looked at my husband and told him, 'You know what we're not going to do? We're not going to cry. We're not going to make the short time we have with him about sadness. We're going to make it about happiness and love. We're going to smile. We're going to remember his face. We're going to hold his little fingers and little toes and just take him in, every second of it. Even though it's just going to be a few minutes, we're going to live in it like it's everything it's supposed to be, that it's not fucked up, that we're happy and whole. Because he's not here to fuel sadness. Once we let him go, that's when we can let the sadness in.' And that's exactly what we did. And I've been in that sadness ever since, and I'm not sure I see a way out of it, and I can barely move, but I do need to buy some food so I don't just rot on my couch—have you ever tried this Stouffer's chicken pot pie? Is it good?"

That's my real answer to their question. But there's absolutely no way that's what they want to hear. It's too real. It's too much. It's authentic to the point of pain. They want to have a role in the story, not be drowning in the mud alongside me. They want to act out the tragedy, not live it.

It would honestly be unfair of me to trauma-dump all of that on them—but they asked. So that's our big lesson from this chapter, friends: don't ask questions you don't want the answers to. Don't force us to lie. Don't make us read the script.

In a way, the script of well-intentioned words is evidence that we're all humans with empathy. If you didn't have empathy, the script wouldn't matter. You wouldn't be affected by someone else's pain. But you are. You are an empathetic, kind person who has the capacity to be rocked by someone else's grief. So you defend yourself. You hold up that script as a shield so you don't have to say, I can't imagine the pain you're in, and I don't want to. Please don't tell me the truth. Please keep your pain to yourself.

And you know what? That's okay.

True support doesn't mean you have to share someone's pain. It doesn't mean you have to dive into the mud with them.

True support is simply throwing away the script.

Throw it out. Don't demand their lines from them. Don't make them stand in that spotlight.

How about just sitting with them in silence? Or speaking your own truth: "I can't imagine what you're going through, but I'm here for you."

Those are just examples. I can't tell you what to say, because I'm not you—and true support is authentic. It comes from you. It can't come from anywhere else.

Most importantly, you have to want to support. It is work. It does take effort. You might not be able to do this right away with every human. But you can choose your humans and practice. You just have to want to.

"LOOKING BACK, WE'LL LAUGH AT THIS..."

In case you haven't figured it out yet, I have a pretty dark and dry sense of humor. (But also realistic and optimistic—I'm not a dark cloud.)

And thank god I do, or some of the shit I heard in the "at least..." category would have put me into a coma.

I do really think that laughter is the only way we find our path out of the darkness. The moment I started cracking up at the insane well-intentioned words I was hearing after Jacob's death was the moment I knew I'd be okay.

So let's take a moment and break the ice. It's okay to laugh! (Actually, I hope you laugh, because otherwise... [TK]) Here are some of the greatest hits from the "at least..." category.

At least you'll get your body back faster! If you were actually pregnant for nine months, it would take way longer. Why thank you, Sandra, I appreciate the concern for my appearance in this trying time.

At least he was only five months old, and you didn't get the chance to really know him. Spot on, Dave. I'm very lucky that I'll never get to talk to my son.

At least you know you can get pregnant. OMG yes, Erica! Exactly! Thank god I know I can keep making babies, only to experience their soul-crushing early deaths!

At least you didn't breastfeed, so your boobs are still nice. What is everyone's obsession with my boobs during times of crisis?

And my absolute favorite, an all-time banger:

At least you already have all the baby stuff, so you won't have to buy it next time. YUP. I literally fall to my knees in gratitude multiple times a day that I either get to keep walking past the constant reminders of my dead child all over my house, or put myself through the laugh riot of boxing up all the gear for the baby we didn't bring home from the hospital.

At the time, each of those "at least"s was delivered by someone who truly, emphatically, completely would have said they were trying to support me.

And I know for sure that if they're reading this right now, they're mortified beyond belief. (My cousin Charlotte said I could call her out by name in this book, so hi, Charlotte, and maybe let's talk sometime about your fixation with my boobs.)

So let's clear the air.

Number one: don't be mortified. It's okay. You have some work to do on your emotional support skills, and being mortified in the first place shows that you care enough to do that work.

Number two: I'm okay. No lasting damage. Would have loved not to hear those zingers in the moment and be short-circuited by rage, but hey, it's water under the bridge and we can laugh about it now.

Number three: after reading this chapter, what would you have said differently?

What would true support have looked like?

Again, it's an answer only you can give, because it has to come authentically from you. So ask yourself: what would it look like to drop the script? What would you say? What would you do?

If you can reflect on those questions and come up with answers that are true to you, then congratulations! You're officially out of the woods. You're going to build better relationships and go deeper into the ones you already have. You're going to be a better friend, partner, sibling, parent, boss (because let's be honest, sometimes they fuck it up the most), or even just acquaintance.

You're going to be a true support to the people you care about.

And "at least..." you'll never fucking say that again.

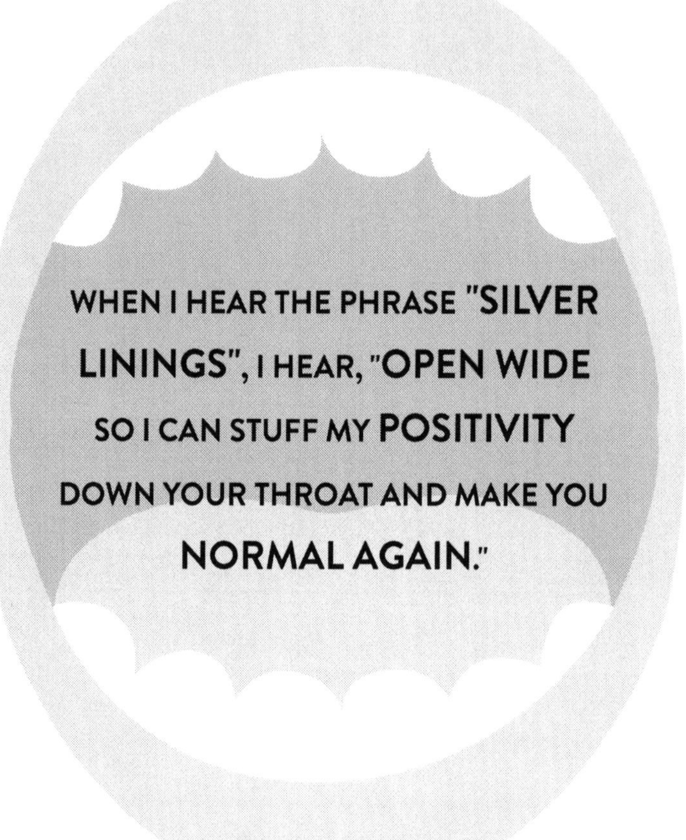

WHEN I HEAR THE PHRASE "SILVER LININGS", I HEAR, "OPEN WIDE SO I CAN STUFF MY POSITIVITY DOWN YOUR THROAT AND MAKE YOU NORMAL AGAIN."

CH*PTER TWO

THERE ARE NO SILVER LININGS IN THE PAIN CAVE

I am not a positive person.

Does this mean I'm a bummer? No. Does it mean I'm out there killing the vibe at every party I'm invited to? Hell no.

Now, I'm not saying I'm the life of the party. Everyone who knows me would agree—that's not me. I have crazy social anxiety, and it takes at least two drinks to really get me warmed up for group fun. But once I'm comfortable, I'm good to go.

And if you've ever seen me goofing off in between sets at the Her Well Wisher gyms I run, then you'd know exactly the kind of fun I like to bring at all times.

But I'm not positive. I hate positive. (If you like to think of yourself as a positive person, I don't hate you, I just hate your positivity.)

Why? Well, because it's not real.

Positivity, in my view, is a performance. And I don't want to put on a performance—and I certainly don't want to have to watch someone else put one on.

I see positivity as wallpapering over reality. Bad things happen, and instead of authentically reacting and feeling our way through it, "being positive" means putting on a mask and ignoring the internal processing that really needs to be done.

This works double when it's someone forcing positivity on you. Like in the wake of some real honest-to-god shit going down in your life.

You're in a pain cave, surrounded by darkness, confused and knocked off your feet by the suddenness of the trauma you're experiencing. All you want to do is get your bearings. It's hard to breathe. It's hard to see. Are you worried at that moment about putting a smile on your face? Hell no—to me, it feels like literally just trying to put one foot in front of the other and get through the day. You're weeks out from smiling. You're focused on surviving.

And then a well-intentioned "ally" spots you and makes it their mission to force that smile out of you.

"Look on the bright side," they say. "There's a silver lining to everything."

Oh really, is there? (If you're trying to clock my tone, think Kristen Wiig drunk on a plane in Bridesmaids.)

Is there, Charlotte?! (Sorry, Charlotte. But you know you do this.)

Positivity is poison when you're deep in tragedy. It feels like a lie. I don't want to look on any bright side, you're thinking. There is no bright side. There is no silver lining to this.

So, no, I'm not a positive person. I want to be truly, wholly myself in every moment. I want to authentically connect in each and every interaction. Even if it's just by saying, "This sucks. Wow, I feel for you. This is awful."

Believe me, hearing those words—a validation of your pain—when you're in a bad place really, really helps. Because even while you're in the pain cave, you're also very conscious of the energy you're putting out. You're very aware of the dark cloud that hangs over your head like a toxic fume. You don't want to spread it around, and you don't want other people to look at you funny. There's an odd self-consciousness and insecurity that comes with being The Sad One. Having someone walk up to you and tell you to "think positive" feels like them saying, "Your sadness is really freaking us out, can you stop? Can you just get over this and be you again?"

Whereas someone simply living in the reality of your pain cave with you, acknowledging how much it sucks, not trying to change it or change you, not trying to erase what you're going through, feels like a relief. Thank god; I'm not crazy. I'm not overreacting. This really does suck. The pain I'm feeling is appropriate.

I'm not a positive person. I'm an optimistic person.

Optimism is kind of like positivity, only without all the wallpapering-over-reality stuff. To be optimistic is to look around in the pain cave and say, "Wow, what a dank, shitty, cold, pitch-black space we're in. This sucks. Let's hold hands and try to slowly make it out together."

It's acknowledging reality, and also acknowledging that together, we can look forward to a brighter future. All things will get better with time, and they'll get better even faster if we give each other the real, authentic support we need.

Optimism feels like action. Whereas positivity? That feels like standing still and ignoring the truth about what you're dealing with.

Which brings me to the well-intentioned words of this chapter: the dreaded silver linings.

I DON'T WANT YOUR ALTERNATE REALITY

You've heard this one a million times, and it's one of the hardest well-intentioned words to clap back to, because it comes from such a desperate place.

People who talk about silver linings are desperate to wallpaper over your reality.

They simply do not want to entertain the notion that a reality could exist in which you're going through the shit you're going through.

Why? I don't know for sure, but I could take some guesses. (Prepare for some vast overgeneralization, and don't hold it against me—I'm just trying to paint a picture here.)

Let's talk about people who grew up in those "happy" households where everyone had to put on a positive face and no one was allowed to acknowledge anything bad that happened. No one was ever angry, no one was ever sad, and life was perfect. (Anyone who did feel sad or angry...

well, they'd better keep it to themselves.)

You probably knew people like that growing up, or you yourself grew up in one of those families. Families where emotions were not allowed. Where everyone had to put on a performance, or they'd be seen as a boat-rocker, or "selfish", or "dramatic".

As adults, those people tend to be Silver Linings people. And I get it—they were trained to find the happy, or else. I do have sympathy for that.

But now, when they're confronted with something terrible happening, they try like hell to spin it to their happy alternate reality. They create "silver linings" to make it seem like it's actually a good thing that this terrible thing happened to you.

Like: "Well, the silver lining is that you wouldn't have Jax if you hadn't lost Jakob."

(YUP. That really happened. Let that soak in for a second—someone really said that.)

In case you were wondering, losing a child isn't something that can be canceled out. Ever. It stays with you like a scar, long after the open, bleeding wound has slowly stitched itself back together. Sometimes I have to remind myself that the scar isn't actually visible on the outside, tracing its jagged edge across my skin for everyone to see. Because that's how real it feels for me.

Having Jax didn't take that scar away. Nothing ever will.

And the last thing a mother who's already lost one child wants to think about is an alternate reality in which it's actually a good thing that her child died.

This is why silver linings hurt so much to hear. They're taking the deep, gut-wrenching pain you went through, the internal battle (and sometimes external, as we'll talk about in the next section) you fought so hard, and turning it into something worthwhile, a game you won, an accomplishment you can be proud of.

Silver linings make the shit you went through "worth it". Worth what, exactly?

Was having Jax worth all the pain I went through in losing Jakob?

How the fuck do I even begin to think about answering such a fucked-up question?

I get that the pain cave is hard. I get that my dark cloud is wafting your way, and the toxicity is threatening to you. I get that you'd rather everything just be sunny and happy and normal again.

But guess what—it's not.

And I don't want your alternate reality. Because that alternate reality is one where the death of my son was a good thing. I don't even want to think about that reality. Get it away from me.

When I hear the phrase "silver linings", I hear, "Open wide so I can stuff my positivity down your throat and make you normal again."

For someone ultra-realistic like me, this is the worst. This isn't support. This isn't love. This is the opposite. It's telling me I'm wrong. Broken. Ugly. That you don't want the version of me that's going through pain. That you think it's your job to force me into feeling better... or you don't want me in your reality.

You know what? I'm actually fine over here in the pain cave. Because the pain cave exists in the same reality where Jakob existed. And that's where I want to be.

I think this is something people forget when they're trying to be positive, trying to wallpaper over reality with silver linings: most of the time, the tough things that happen to us involve the loss of something we loved and cherished.

A child. A spouse. A job. Our health. Our marriage.

We lost something. We're grieving that loss.

"What is grief, if not love persevering?" is a question I heard once on TV, and that line says it all. Grief only exists because love existed.

Don't try to take away my grief. Don't try to create a reality in which my grief doesn't exist.

It's a reality in which the thing I love, the thing I lost, didn't exist either. And that's not a place I want to be.

LET US FIGHT OUR BATTLES

After I lost Jakob, I went to war with myself.

See, it hadn't been just a fluke that he died—part of the problem was my body.

At age 28, I went in for a routine pap smear and came out

with a diagnosis of cervical dysplasia. It was "late stage", which basically meant, "you're not going to have to wait months to get in with a specialist". By the time I even caught up with what was happening, I was having a series of procedures to remove the precancerous cells that ended up causing, as we discovered years later when pregnant with Jakob, an "incompetent cervix".

Having to hand over my dead son to the nurses and watch him be taken away forever wasn't even the end of the story in that particularly hellish chapter of my life. Physically, I was not okay. Part of the placenta had remained attached. I hemorrhaged and got extremely sick. I had to have emergency surgery.

And then suddenly, all my vitals were finally at normal levels again. The wounds that had ripped their way through my body were no longer life-threatening. In what felt like a millisecond, I was discharged as though it was "over".

Before I knew it, I was buckled into the passenger's seat of our car. I was supposed to go home. But I'd entered that hospital with a baby inside me, and I was supposed to leave with one in my arms. Sitting in our car, my husband Brian patiently waiting for me to give the go-ahead to pull away from the curb, I was paralyzed. Frozen. I couldn't leave. It seemed insane to me that I would simply drive away from the only place I had ever held my son, leave him and those memories behind, and just get on with life.

In the aftermath, I hated my body for not hanging on to my son. I was so angry at it. How could you fuck up like this? How could you lose your baby?

The only thing that brought me any comfort was doling out punishment to the responsible party, so that's what I did. I went into the gym and started working out. And I didn't stop. I worked out to a toxic level, pushing my body past effort and into pain, making it pour sweat and shake with fatigue. You weren't strong enough, I thought, and so I was determined to whip my body into the strongest it could possibly be, even if it hurt to do so. I wanted the pain, actually; it was easier to feel the physical punishment than it was to feel the jagged, bleeding hole in my heart where Jakob's memory was.

When I got pregnant again with Jax, it wasn't like the first time with Jakob. Women who have been through miscarriages and child loss know this all too well. The second time, you're just waiting for the hammer to drop. You're waiting to wake up bleeding and cramping, knowing it's over. You're afraid to let yourself feel happiness because it might get snatched away from you again, and you remember the pain that nearly killed you the first time.

It seemed like people in my life understood the fragile state we were in while I was pregnant with Jax, because I didn't hear a lot of well-intentioned words during that time. It was like everyone, including me and Brian, was holding their breath. I went on bed rest at 14 weeks (believe it or not, it is possible to watch too much Friends) and, thankfully, Jax held on in there until 29 weeks—early enough to be a "miracle baby" and need 3 months in the NICU, but alive and healthy.

And when Jax was born? Oh boy, did people let out that breath they'd been holding, and start word-vomiting at me the silver linings that apparently surrounded us on all sides.

I think people love to believe that everything is planned.

That everything has a reason. That we aren't all just along for an unpredictable ride on a chaos roller coaster hurtling uncontrollably through space and time. They need to feel the illusion that someone, or something, is in control.

So, when Jax was born? "This really shows the silver lining—you wouldn't have Jax if you hadn't lost Jakob."

Yes, of course, why didn't I think of that? Never mind on that whole child loss thing; lifelong grief = cured!

When Jax had to stay in the NICU, and we were in the hospital every day for 3 months? "The silver lining here is you're prepared, after what you went through with your last pregnancy."

Totally. Totally. I feel totally confident and prepped for our entire lives to revolve around a tiny incubator and machines in a hospital room.

When we were finally able to bring Jax home? "Hey, silver lining—he's already on a great schedule from being with the nurses for so long!"

Holy shit, you're right! Watching a series of strangers performing basic mothering tasks for a baby I could only hold for brief periods of time wasn't at all an identity crisis for a traumatized new mom.

Each new silver lining only added to the internal monologue my brain was starting to repeat over and over like a mantra:

You're not strong enough. You're taking this too hard. You shouldn't be in this much pain.

Every time someone threw a new alternate reality in my face, it was like they were telling me I just needed to get over it, move on, go back to normal.

But in my reality, I was still in a battle. I was still fighting. I was fighting to work my way through grief, fear, physical trauma, and anxiety that sent me spiraling into PTSD. PTSD so strong that most days, I wanted to return the baby. "He can't be here. Take him back." I was fighting to be the best mom I could. And I was fighting to get my feet under me, to feel strong and confident again, in a body that had almost failed two children.

You know how they say that if you help a baby bird break out of its shell, you kill it? It needs the struggle of working its way out of the egg to build up the muscles that will ensure it can survive. It needs to go through the battle, or it will die.

That's what we need, too, when we're battling our way through healing in the pain cave.

Let us fight our battles. It's the only way we're going to survive on the other side.

And what if, instead of pretending the battle doesn't exist... you acknowledge that we're fighting it, and back us up in the fight?

THE RIGHT THING TO SAY

I said in Chapter One that I'm not going to tell you what to say.

I do hope you're never going to try to "find the silver lining" again, though. I hope you're going to acknowledge

"There have been many highs and lows with my breast cancer journey. I struggled with body image after my cancer diagnosis and especially after my DMX (double mastectomy). There are still days I fight to recognize my body, to appreciate my scars, and to remind myself what my body went through to fight against cancer.

The most difficult reaction or comment I have heard several times was, "At least you get a free boob job?" Oh sure, a free boob job with a side of cancer? I have heard this several times and what they assume is that I want a 'boob job.' Do they assume I need one in order to feel like a woman or are they simply trying to make light of the conversation? Regardless, a comment like that is not needed or welcomed.

I think the number one gift you can give someone going through cancer is your genuine presence, your quiet time, and a listening ear. Sometimes saying nothing at all is saying everything! Every cancer survivor is worthy of body love while healing and long after."

JAMIE

the pain cave instead of pretending it's not there. I hope you're going to keep your "positivity" to yourself, and just be okay with meeting someone where they are, even if that place is dark, painful, and scary.

I can't tell you what to say, because it needs to come from you.

But you know what I would have loved to hear, at any point, throughout the whole long struggle between losing Jakob and bringing home Jax?

"Who did he look like—you or Brian?"

Great question. And yes, let's talk about him! Let's talk about Jakob. He was real. He existed. I would love to tell you about him. I would love to paint a picture of my son, who I loved a lifetime's worth in a just a few short hours. He was amazing. I would love for you to know just how amazing.

Grief is just love, after all—love, in a different form. It's all the love we felt and now have nowhere to put. All this love, bottled up inside, trying to tear its way out of you, and it has nowhere to go. That's what makes it so painful.

So give us somewhere to put our grief. Don't avoid talking about what we lost—let's talk about it!

I love the reality where Jakob was real. I want to invite you into it. Because even though it's painful, it's worth all the pain. There's so much love in it. Let's share that. Let's not erase it.

Let's talk about him.

That's what real support looks like: living into our world with us, being there with us, even though it's painful and messy. Holding our hand in the pain cave and just existing with us.

Don't be afraid to climb in and get comfortable.

(By the way... he looked exactly like Brian.)

NOBODY WINS IN A WORLD WHERE WE'RE ALL FUELED BY **TOXIC JUDGMENT** AND **SHAMING** OTHERS.

CH*PTER THREE

SHAMING ISN'T CARING

You ever have one of those interactions that makes you want to slap someone right across the face?

(At this point in the book, I feel the need to express that I'm really a very calm, kind person and rarely resort to physical violence. Except in my head, when someone crosses a line—then it's on.)

You know what I'm talking about—those interactions where someone is all up in your business, asking questions, dropping not-so-subtle hints about what you should be doing in your tragic circumstances.

"Are you sure you should..." or "Wouldn't it be better to..."

They're doing it under the guise of caring about you, but what they're really doing is judging.

I got a lot of this when we finally came home from the hospital with Jax.

Actually, rewind: I got a lot of this when we were *still in the hospital with Jax.* Remember how I said it felt like everyone was holding their breath while I was pregnant with him, and then once he was out, it was like the dam broke?

The waters behind that dam ran deep with judgment. *Everyone* had something to say about our situation, and most of their thoughts were super judgmental. Of me. Of how I was reacting, behaving, *living* as a new mom with a baby in the NICU. And before you say I was being dramatic and paranoid in my traumatized postpartum state, I know for a fact they were being judgmental. Because they'd say it to me, straight up.

"You must feel so tired."

"You must feel so anxious not having him home."

"You must feel relieved that you at least get to sleep through the night, though, right?"

Couple things. One, *you have no idea how I'm feeling.* Stop projecting your assumptions and thinly veiled judgments on me.

Second: I don't really feel anything. I'm numb. (Hint: when someone says they're numb, don't talk about feelings. Just give. Just try to fill them back up where they're empty.)

The only people who *really* knew how I felt were the other moms in the NICU. It was like a little club, the worst kind of club—but we all supported each other in solidarity. One of us would come into the NICU and collapse in a chair, take a huge heaving sigh, and say, "Thank god. Just us in here. I don't have to deal with anyone else." It was our safe haven; no one could infiltrate us in there. It was a little bubble of cheerleading and commiseration and validation.

And every time we left that room, everyone in the outside world just kept lobbing the judgment grenades at our faces.

It didn't just feel like judgment; it felt like *shaming.*

And that's what this chapter is about. Because weirdly enough, going through tough times tends to invite a *lot* of shaming. Everyone has an opinion, and everyone thinks they know best what you should be doing and feeling and thinking.

Nothing you do is good enough. You're just trying to survive... but you're doing survival *wrong*. The problem is, everyone's version of "right" is different. And you're the one taking hit after hit as the full weight of everyone's opinions come flying at you like a firing squad.

What the hell is going on?

PREVENTION THROUGH INVENTION

Ask any mom about our society's shaming culture, and they'll be able to rattle off more than a dozen stories about the toxic shame-riddled bullshit they've been fed at some point during their motherhood journey.

Some of the worst shaming is mom-on-mom violence—we're so conditioned to shame women for every damn thing they do, we're even shaming each other!

Those moms at your organized playgroups? They have a lot to say about the snacks you're feeding your kid and how they would *never* feed their little angel a GMO peanut or whatever the hell is this week's food villain. Those mommy groups on Facebook? There be monsters. Enter at your own peril. There is literally nothing you can say that won't be met with pearl-clutching and horrified judgment. "I notice your baby has a Sophie in this photo...Sophie the Giraffe is FULL OF TOXIC MOLD THAT WILL GIVE YOUR BABY A BRAIN TUMOR!!1" It's enough to make a new mom have a panic attack (for the fifth time that day, because having a newborn is just like that).

You'd think moms, many of whom have gone through the intense physical upheaval and vulnerability of pregnancy and childbirth, and all of whom experience the joy of lying awake at night in terror, ruminating on everything that can go wrong at any moment once the baby's born, would have more grace for each other. So where does this intense shaming come from?

If I'm looking at it through the lens of generous intent—which, despite my earlier daydreams of slapping the shit out of certain people, is how I prefer to operate at all times—I can forgive the shaming, because I can tell it comes from a very human place: fear.

Yes, fear. We're all afraid that something bad will happen

to us or the people we love. When you're a mom, this is multiplied by incalculable billions. Mom anxiety is both hilariously irrational (raise your hand if you ever googled "can I accidentally poop out the baby" when pregnant) and *all too real.* It can be crushing.

So when you're presented with the opportunity to pass judgment on a supposed "mistake" someone else is making... it feels like you're actually preventing yourself from making that same mistake.

If you just invent a reality in which you know everything you're not supposed to do—in which you're the authority on keeping your kid safe—then you can prevent anything bad from happening, right?

This is what I think is going on with all the shaming, both mom-on-mom and in general. People want to invent a reality where nothing can touch them because they know everything and can therefore prevent disaster. Prevention through invention.

When you're feeling low, getting a few moments of perceived superiority over someone else helps boost you just a little bit.

Well, here's the problem with that.

It's a race to the bottom.

You might feel better for a split second by passing judgment on someone else's inorganic baby food or death trap of a crib setup, but that feeling is fleeting, and the original fear is still there.

And now the person you passed judgment on feels like shit. And to feel better, they pass on that judgment to someone else. It just keeps going and going, like a chain reaction. When the judgment stops doing the job to make you feel better, you start multiplying the toxicity with a friend—you sit and judge others, shitting on everyone else, making up multipliers like "everything happens in threes". (Of course a third bad thing is going to happen when you're looking for it!)

Nobody wins in a world where we're all fueled by toxic judgment and shaming others. It stops making you feel better. It only goes so far. It starts seeping into your bones and your blood. It does things to you.

Pretty soon we're left with a world where everyone feels desperately inadequate and nobody has the support they need.

WISH HER WELL

Years ago, a friend and I were talking about how women really need to be better to each other. We were both going through rough stuff at the time. We lit on the same brilliant idea at the same time, a phrase that I could never have imagined would take on such significance in my life and the lives of so many others:

"Before you say anything, wish her well."

It's a little mental trick I would play to make sure I was sending out the most supportive, loving energy I could to each woman who would come into my gym (now multiple gyms, all under the Her Well Wisher umbrella—I told you it would become hugely significant). I decided I would be a well-wisher for every woman I saw, because every

"The sharpest pain I've ever felt has been specifically as a parent. I think the fundamental expression of support I so desperately needed from loved ones was curiosity. I needed someone to say "Tell me." At my height of pain, it's not dramatic to say I was in an existential crisis, experiencing a total dissociation from everything I loved about myself and my life.

Shame and loneliness are everywhere. Trauma in the mundane abounds, especially in our increasingly disconnected and fragile systems of society. I try to ask and not tell, even when assumptions that I know exactly what somebody is going through feel strong and certain. And, when it turns out my assumptions were right, it is an absolute delight to connect and share more about me. But I am humbled to recognize how often my assumptions are actually off, and to know how hurtful my "knowing" could have been.

Curiosity is connection and acceptance. Curiosity is love."

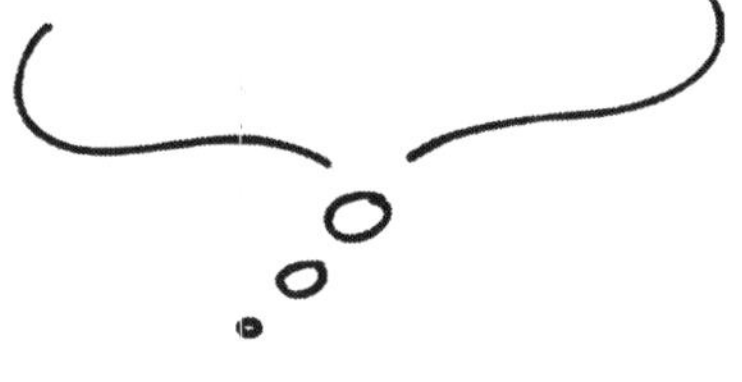

ANNE

woman needs one. The best way to be an ally to women is to fundamentally change your view of them as one based on compassion, kindness and love.

Our society is an absolute judgment *minefield* for women. We're trained from the time we're kids to scrutinize women: how they dress, how they talk, how they behave, how they choose to live their lives. We're taught that they need to meet an impossible standard, or they're failing. It's so insidious that you have girls as young as six going on diets and women as young as 20 getting "preventative" Botox and fillers. Scroll social media, and you'll see post after post perpetuating the mass cultural evisceration of whichever female celebrity we've decided to tear down that week.

It's absolutely insane. It can drive someone crazy. (It's a big reason I try to stay off social media.)

You might think you don't do this, but maybe you've seen someone else do it. You know, like when you were a kid at the store with your mom, and you'd see tabloids screaming things like, "WHO WORE IT BETTER" and "BEACH BODY BEST AND WORST", and you'd see your mom actually pick it up and look at it—and worse, repeat things like that later at home. Looking at herself in the mirror and sighing, saying something bad about herself. Unknowingly passing on a generation wound to the little girl watching her, even when she thinks she's just talking to herself.

Are you sure you don't do the same thing today? Here's a question: ever filtered a photo on Instagram? Ever done it in front of your daughter? It seems so innocent, but what she's seeing through a child's eyes is pretty simple: you aren't comfortable with the world seeing you as you really are. You fear their judgment. *She should fear their judgment.* She grows up with that fear, and it infects her just like your own mom's reaction to the tabloids. (Imagine if we just got rid of all the filters entirely—the world would be so much healthier. Then again, I wonder what else we'd come up with to replace our endless need to judge and shame women simply for existing.)

When I first opened my gym, I was attracting a mostly female clientele. Gyms are environments that can be filled with self-judgment and self-consciousness for women; there are mirrors, there are other people with "better bodies", and you can find yourself constantly looking around feeling dread at how much you don't "measure up" to the other women. You know, because you've been trained by society, that you're constantly being judged.

So I made it off limits at my gym.

"When you see another woman, before you say anything to her or about her, take a moment in your head to wish her well. Wish her a good day. Wish her good health and happiness." This was the mantra I'd teach at my gym.

When you wish someone well, it does something funny: it short-circuits any judgment you could possibly have about them.

A woman walks by wearing super-short gym shorts. *She doesn't have the ass to wear those,* you might reflexively think in your head, and really you're talking about *yourself,* and you know it, but you still think it because that's how our society has trained us to look at women.

If you can catch yourself before thinking it, though, and insert a well-wish, it changes everything.

You see the same woman walk by and your first thought is, I hope she's having a great day. I hope she feels happy. I hope she's enjoying her walk.

Once you've wished her well, *the judgment doesn't follow.* It's really hard to feel judgmental toward someone you've just wished well.

So that's our mantra. *Wish her well.* Before you think or say anything, wish her well. Any judgment, any negativity, evaporates.

The chain reaction, the race to the bottom, stops with you.

Something I discovered when working with so many women at Her Well Wisher was something I knew deep down, because it was also my experience:

Usually, the woman they needed to wish well the most was themselves.

The training we get on judging and shaming women starts with judging and shaming ourselves. It's almost a reflex. You see yourself in the mirror: *Ugh, I look like shit today.*

You see a photo of yourself: *God, do I really look like that in that outfit?* You go clothes shopping: *Nothing fits. I need to lose weight.*

What if every time you saw yourself in the mirror, you took a pause before the judgment and wished her well first?

What if you made it a point to be your own well-wisher?

It's amazing how little judgment you can find for yourself once you've wished yourself well. Try it. It works.

THE WORST MOM IN THE WORLD

"How can you stand to go home, knowing your son is at the hospital? I could never do that."

If you're shocked, I don't blame you. But yeah. That was a *very* common question. The number of times I got asked this when Jax was in the NICU was directly proportional to the number of times I daydreamed about smacking someone.

Thank you *so* much for reminding me yet again about the single hardest thing I've ever had to do, and the fact that I have to do it every day for three months!

When Jax was born, I'd already had the crushing paralysis of entering the hospital with a baby and having to drive away without one. It was a traumatic moment that cut a hole in me. It carved off a piece of my soul. I was never the same after that. And when Jax was delivered early at 29 weeks, and he needed to stay in the NICU, I was faced with the exact same scenario: I was going to have to drive away from the hospital without my baby.

Over. And over. And over.

Imagine the most traumatic moment of your life. Now

imagine having to relive it every single day for three months.

It wrecked me. Brian and I would be at the hospital all day with Jax, holding his tiny hands and watching him breathe with the assistance of machines. We'd eat there. We'd take naps there. At first, I thought very seriously of figuring out how I could live there.

But obviously, that wasn't possible. We had to go home each day. We had to do all the regular things you have to do to take care of yourself: shower, grocery shop, clean the house. We had to live, even though our baby was in a hospital away from us.

It had only been about a week of this soul-crushing existence when I got that question for the first time. "How do you drive away each night, knowing your baby isn't with you?"

Of course I know they didn't mean to hurt me, but there is not a question on earth that could have cut me deeper. Of course I know they were just curious and sympathetic and trying to relate to what I was experiencing, but all I heard over and over in my head was, *You drove away without Jakob. Now you're driving away without Jax. You're the worst mom in the world.*

This was compounded, of course, by all the usual mom shaming. It started with breastfeeding. (If you're a mom, I know you're wincing and nodding sympathetically right now.)

People, let's get something straight: *don't tell a mom she needs to be breastfeeding.* In fact, just don't mention breastfeeding at all.

If you're not a parent, you might not know how incredibly touchy this subject is, how divisive it can be, and how brutally judgmental people can get. And by people, I don't just mean other moms. I mean nurses. I mean doctors.

"You have a preemie. He needs breast milk. He needs all that goodness only you can give him. You need to try harder. You need to breastfeed. Why aren't you breastfeeding? Isn't that what's best for him?"

Well, actually, Charlotte, the only time he managed to

latch on he ended up needing to be resuscitated (by me!!), so no, I'm not exactly sure it *is* what's best for him. I feel like being *alive* is what's best for him. I feel like *breathing* is probably the key priority.

Also, why the hell do you care?

That's the question I wanted to scream at everyone who had something to say about the way I was mothering a 29-week preemie who needed machines to stay alive. *Why do you care? What is it to you how I go about keeping my son alive? Can't you see that I'm doing my fucking best even though I'm a quivering mass of trauma myself?*

I wasn't producing enough milk, and I got told it was because I wasn't feeding him enough. *So sorry I'm slacking,* I thought. I started pumping constantly. I became a shell of an Angry Horrible Woman who wasn't getting the serotonin from having her baby naturally breastfeed. Pumping was awful. My production went down even more. I stopped pumping, and the doctors said, "You have to pump. It's essential for Jax to have breast milk."

You can't imagine what saying that does to a mom who's

already held one dead child in her arms. I was a basket case. I lost my mind trying to pump. Trying to do it right. Trying not to be the Worst Mom in the World.

After another month of this, with my anxiety burning hotter than the sun and my mental health in shreds, Brian put his foot down. "You're not doing this anymore. We're going to the hospital and they're going to tell us how to not do it anymore. This is not life."

He was right, of course, and guess what happened when *he* said that to the doctors? Magically, another solution was found.

By the time we got to bring Jax home, I was, to put it lightly, Not Doing Well. Mentally. I had been through so much and hadn't taken a moment to try to sort through it all—I was in Preemie Mom mode.

Boy, those well-intentioned words just kept on coming.

Let's run through some greatest hits. First, an "at least...":

At least with a preemie you weren't pregnant long enough

to get stretch marks.

Ugh, *so* spot on, Jessica—my son's lungs were underdeveloped jelly that required an army of machines to keep him alive, but I am going to turn heads at the beach this summer!

Had a few choice Silver Linings, too:

Hey, silver lining: you get to take more time off work!

Totally. *Totally*. Wow, Kyle. You couldn't be more right. I love not making money and contemplating financial ruin while watching my son struggle to make it through each day.

The judgment didn't stop with breastfeeding, either. When we brought Jax home, we were warned by the doctors that his immune system was incredibly vulnerable and that we had to be really strict about who came near him.

Oh, don't tell me you're one of those moms who doesn't let anyone touch her baby...

Hand sanitizer? I'm not even touching him; I feel like you're overreacting...

Uh oh, we've got a helicopter mom in the making!

Shit, you're right, I forgot that you getting to have two minutes of face time with a cute baby is more important than that baby not dying from a common cold! My bad! Here, sneeze all over him! Give him a lick! Who cares, right? It's just germs, what did a germ ever do to a baby?

I turned into a defensive linebacker when it came to Jax. "Yeah, you *bet* I'm one of those moms," I'd say, trying to keep the tone playful but making sure to put enough steel in my voice that they knew I meant business.

Because by that point, I'd been through so much with my kids that I wasn't going to let the mommy shaming take me down. You want to shame me? Go ahead. You want to shame moms who won't let anyone near their immune-compromised preemies? Weird, but get after it. Rock on with your self-centered, antisocial self. Preemie moms can take it. We've already been through the worst thing imaginable: driving away from a hospital every night knowing in the back of your mind that there's a chance your baby won't be alive when you come back tomorrow.

There's nothing worse than that. You want to shame us so you can feel better about the things that haunt you in the middle of the night, the things you think you can prevent if you can summon five seconds of superiority over someone else?

Go ahead.

Or, how about this?

Don't.

Because those things that haunt you—they aren't any less likely to happen to you just because you shamed someone who they *did* happen to.

That's that pesky lack of control coming back around. We can't control what happens to us. I couldn't control losing Jakob. I couldn't control Jax being premature.

We get to make a choice in each moment: to react to our lack of control with fear and judgment and shaming, or to react with acceptance. Just acceptance.

I had to look in the mirror each morning before driving back to the hospital to see Jax and, before all the self-loathing and judgment came flooding in, wish the woman I saw in the mirror well.

She needed that. She needed someone wishing her well.

So do all the women in your life.

I think, at the end of the day, that we can all be better allies to the women in our lives. And we, as women, can all be better allies to ourselves.

Instead of a race to the bottom, we can be a rising tide that lifts all boats.

We can make her feel like the *best* mom in the world.

We can make her feel like she's doing great. That she's going to be fine. That everything is going to work out okay.

We can wish her well.

CHAPTER THREE

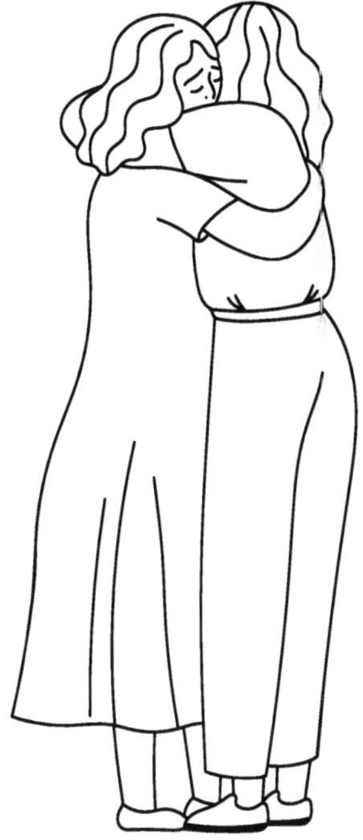

REMEMBER: IT'S NOT ABOUT YOU. DECENTER YOURSELF. THIS IS ABOUT THEM, AND THEY'LL TELL YOU WHAT THEY NEED IF YOU MAKE IT EASY.

CH*PTER FOUR

"HAVE YOU TRIED...?"

When you're in the grip of a tough time, when you're stressed, when you're desperate, when you're barely hanging on... you would do anything to feel normal again.

Which means you *try* everything to feel normal again. You want to find something, anything, that will make things start to get easier.

You scour the internet for strangers' advice. You read books (or listen to them, as I used to do while taking newborn Jax for walks in his stroller). You listen to podcasts. You obsessively hunt down every avenue of potential solutions, because you're exhausted and so sick of feeling that way. You want to live again.

So many women I know have gone through this with sleep

training their kids. They're absolutely beside themselves trying to find something that will make the baby *go the fuck to sleep.* They try every solution that can possibly be scraped out of the internet, no matter how crazy it sounds. They haven't had more than three hours of sleep at a time in weeks, maybe even months, and there is truly only so much sleep deprivation the human body can take.

My friend Callie was in such a state back when her daughter was a baby. This kid *would not sleep.* It didn't matter what Callie tried. Cry it out, soothe, Ferber, white noise, nothing worked.

Callie became a zombie. She was starting to experience memory loss. She'd randomly burst into tears. She'd get her daughter down for sleep for a precious few hours, and just as it seemed like actual sleep might be in the cards... the wailing. Always with the wailing, this child.

When Callie was going through this, I was already out of the woods with Jax's rough baby period, and I was in full-blown support mode. I'd get Callie groceries, load and unload her dishwasher, or come over and just hold the baby while Callie took a nap. I knew exactly where she was emotionally and I knew the best thing to do was just take things off her plate and let her rest, so that's what I did.

One day I showed up at Callie's place to find her yelling into her phone at someone. The baby was awake (of course), and just staring placidly at her mom like she was honestly a little impressed.

Callie hung up the phone and threw it on the couch. Her face was red with rage.

"Have I tried this? Have I tried that?!" she yelled. "*Obviously* I've tried everything! Does she think I'm an idiot?"

She was ranting at no one in particular, just venting her frustrations into the air. "Let me guess," I said. "Mom? Or mother in law?"

I was right, it turned out. Her mother in law had called her up once again to give her "advice" on the baby's sleep training. And she did the thing that might be the most infuriating thing you can possibly hear when you're going through a tough time: the mind-blowingly stupid "Have you tried...?"

I didn't blame Callie for exploding. "Have you tried" is like kryptonite. It's a great way to totally waste someone's time while simultaneously calling them stupid.

That being said, it's probably the *most well-intentioned* of the words we'll talk about in this book, so it's really hard to hold it against the person saying it. (Unless it's your mother in law and it's the tenth time she's asked you the same question.)

Let's dive in.

YES, FOR THE LOVE OF GOD, I'VE TRIED

"Have you tried...?" is maddening to hear. It makes your blood boil.

But it's also coming from such a deep instinct in most people: the desire to be the hero, and the belief that they have *the* solution that will take away all your pain.

They really, really want to be the one to save the day. Picture it: you have a friend like Callie who is about to go catatonic from sleep deprivation. Her life is falling apart. Years are being shaved off of her life span. She's Not Doing Good. It's horrible to see her like this, and as someone who loves her, you really want to help her. (You also miss your friend and, a little selfishly, want her back to her old self.)

You're scrolling Instagram one day when you come across something you haven't seen before: a new type of white noise machine that vibrates in the baby's crib while blaring the equivalent of a category 5 hurricane through its little heart-shaped speaker. *Why moms are going crazy for this viral sleep machine*, reads the caption. You see a mountain of comments on the post saying things like, "We would be institutionalized if not for this thing" and "This saved our lives when nothing else worked" and "Sometimes I wonder if my baby has a secret meth addiction but not anymore because HE'S FINALLY ASLEEP".

Hot damn! you think. I did it! I'm about to save the day!

You snap a screenshot of the item and eagerly text it to your zombie-mom friend. *Have you tried this? It's new and everyone is apparently saying it's foolproof!* You feel the glow of accomplishment from knowing you've truly changed a life today.

A few minutes later, your phone buzzes. It's your friend. She has sent back a picture of her own.

It's the "foolproof" sleep machine. In fact, it's three of them, all gifts from well-meaning family and friends. One looks suspiciously like it got thrown against a wall at some point.

Yeah. We tried it. Enough said.

So...no, you didn't save the day. In fact, all you did was require your friend to spend time educating you while biting back the frustration of having to explain for the millionth time to someone that *yes, for the love of God, I've tried.*

"Have you tried" feels like the most helpful thing you could do, because it's offering a solution, engaging in your friend's problem like you're getting in the trenches with them. Unfortunately, in reality, it may actually be the *least* helpful thing you can say. No one wants to have to repeat over and over, as though validating their actions, the things they've already tried to remedy a tough situation. No one going through hell wants to have to recount every step of their journey to prove they've really, truly, tried.

My reaction to the "have you tried" grenade got more and more sarcastic over time until I was actually pretty sure I was pissing people off. But I didn't care. (After losing Jakob, going through hell with Jax, my resulting battle with PTSD, and getting through the newborn and toddler years, I had precisely zero fucks left to give.)

Have I tried? Of *course* I've tried. Do you think I'm sitting on my hands over here? Do you think I don't care enough to try absolutely everything in my power to make things better? Do you think I'm stupid? Do you think I can't handle things on my own?

"Have you tried" manages to be both patronizing and childish at the same time. It's just about the dumbest thing you can say while also inadvertently calling someone stupid.

Here's the thing about offering solutions to someone else's tough time or tragedy. Sometimes, there *is* no solution. In fact, *most of the time* there's no solution.

There's just survival. There's just getting through, and hoping that time will do its thing and heal all wounds, or at least make them hurt less.

Sometimes a situation can't be fixed. It can only be gotten through.

And by trying to fix it, well-intentioned people are actually adding to the load.

When you're supporting someone going through a rough time, the *last* thing you want to do is give them more water to carry. You want to lighten their load, take things off their plate. You want to make things easier, not harder. You want to build them up, not make them even more frustrated.

Give the people in your life the benefit of the doubt. *They've tried it.*

Instead of trying to fix things, trying to be the hero—what if you just showed up? What if you landed on their doorstep and just let them tell you what they need?

DON'T ADD WORK

When life kicks you in the teeth, getting through it is *work.*

It feels like an extra job. It's like you're living a second life

"Finding out you're pregnant after infertility and IVF? Amazing.

Giving birth to your babies at 27 weeks and robbed of that pregnancy? Awful.

We endured 75 and 81 days in the NICU, with lots of bumps along the road. But after those NICU stays, we brought two babies home to love and provide for. It was just different and slightly terrifying, knowing our babies were medically complex and required a lot of needs that a normal baby didn't. Luckily, I was surrounded by dear friends and also other NICU parents who became an incredible support system for what was such a roller coaster ride.

I too struggle to find the words to others going through their own trauma or grief, so I know the love that comes behind well-meaning intentions. But hearing, "At least you can be happy that you didn't have to be 9 months pregnant!" was like a punch in the gut. I would have given anything to endure month nine of a pregnancy, to bring home two babies like I was supposed to have done and care for them.

Sometimes just a simple, "I'm so sorry that sucks" or "What a shitty card to be dealt" feels better than the unintentional reminder of what should have been."

JULIE

of darkness and feeling like shit on top of your "real" life, which is moving forward like nothing happened. You're expected to keep up with both.

After we brought Jax home from the hospital, like I mentioned before, I was Not Okay. The trauma of what I'd been through with both babies was just too much. PTSD hit me like a sledgehammer to the face.

I couldn't leave the house. I didn't want to see anyone. I'd stand next to Jax's crib watching him breathe in his sleep for hours. I had nightmares and couldn't sleep. To this day, I have very few memories of that time (which sucks—but thank god for all the pictures I took on my phone, almost like I knew my suffering brain wasn't able to write down everything I'd want to remember later).

And life went on. Brian was back at work. My friends wanted to catch up and see the baby. Groceries needed to be bought, bills needed to be paid, laundry needed to be done. The world was spinning, but I was stuck.

I do have one persistent memory from that time: pasta.

I had one *very* well-intentioned friend (it's not you this time, Charlotte) who thought she was being really helpful by dropping off pasta salad at my house. All the time. Multiple times a week.

Isn't that what you're supposed to do? you're probably thinking. Just help out, without being asked?

Yes. Definitely. And I did appreciate this friend *not* falling into the anti-helpful "let me know what I can do to help!" trap.

Let you know what you can do to help? Cool, I'll just write that down on my already endless list of shit to do (right between "take out the trash" and "have a mental breakdown") and get to it the thirty-fifth of never.

This friend managed to avoid that, and I was grateful. They showed up. They brought food.

The only problem: I couldn't eat it.

My gut was an absolute mess after years of hormonal roller coasters, hospital stays, and stress. I had to be really careful with everything I ate or I'd immediately get a stomachache. Pasta was off the list, and I didn't have the heart to tell my friend that I couldn't eat any of her kind gesture.

So instead, pasta salad piled up in our fridge until it was overflowing. Meaning I then had to figure out how to squeeze cleaning out the fridge in between everything else I had to do.

Bringing pasta salad to my house was a truly kind gesture—but it wasn't helpful. It added to my work. It put more on my plate, not less.

It was the *performance* of support...but it wasn't actually supportive.

There's a sweet spot in between "let me know what I can do to help" and just showing up with pasta salad, and if possible, it's where you want to land to be a real ally to someone going through a hard time.

"Can I do [insert item] for you?"

See, by making a suggestion of help, you're presenting the premise that *you are going to help.* You're showing up. You're not asking "if" or "how", you're saying, "I'm showing up, and you can count on that." That alone is huge.

But you're not making assumptions about what they need. You're allowing them to agree to help offered, but letting them set the size and shape of it. "Can I get groceries for you?" "No, I use Instacart... but I could use help putting them away and food prepping." Or, "Can I come take care of the yard for you?" "Actually, we have a yard guy who covers that...but could you walk the dog?"

Real help is lightening the load. Taking away the work.

It's not trying to fix things or be the hero; it's not *performing* support. It's just being there. Letting the person who needs help guide, but not making them take charge.

Remember: it's not about you. Decenter yourself. This is about them, and they'll tell you what they need if you make it easy.

OKAY, BUT YOU HAVE TO ACCEPT THE HELP, TOO

Ironically, "have you tried" managed to help me in one big way: it was my training ground for actually expressing myself, being honest about what I needed, and asking for help.

Historically, I was *not* an "ask for help" kind of girl. In fact, people would try to help me and I'd get mad. Don't you dare. I got this. I can take care of myself. Hyper-independent women are that way for a reason—we've been let down so consistently throughout our lives that we've formed a negative cognitive association with asking for help, and the only person we 100% trust to actually get shit done is ourselves.

But during this time, I *had* to get vulnerable. I had to actually accept help. That was step one. Then I had to learn to ask for it. That was step two.

I let people come over to cook for me–previously unheard of, with my clean freak OCD nature. But I had to let them.

I couldn't cook and I needed food. They came over, used my ingredients, and I learned to deal with it.

People offered to walk my dogs. They offered to drive me to the doctor. I had to let them. I couldn't walk further than across the house, and I definitely couldn't drive.

It slowly got easier and easier. I wasn't yet ready to *ask* for help—that muscle wouldn't be built until later on, when I got cancer and all bets were off—but I was able to learn to *accept* help, and that was a big enough step all on its own.

That part is all up to you. People are going to offer help, and you need to work on accepting. Support is a two way street.

HE WAS A BOY WHO COMMITTED SUICIDE. BUT THAT DOESN'T CHANGE WHO HE WAS.

CH*PTER FIVE

WHEN THEY SAY NOTHING AT ALL

Sometimes, there are no words.

I don't just mean in the figurative sense, although that's true, too. It's taken me almost a decade to figure out how to describe some of the tough things I've been through with the right words. Words that convey the loss, grief, and hopelessness. Words that paint a picture of how painful every step I took through every day was.

But with this, I mean it literally: sometimes, people say nothing at all.

No well-intentioned words.

No "at least."

No silver linings.

No attempts to fix the situation. No offerings of solutions.

Sometimes, there's just silence.

CHAPTER FIVE

LET'S TALK ABOUT IT

Okay, let's just get it out of the way. I've wanted to scream this question every day for the past several years since the single worst thing I've ever been through happened.

Why don't we talk about suicide?

We are culturally *weird* about suicide. We treat it like it's contagious. Like it's shameful. Like the person who committed suicide didn't even exist.

We prefer to get through a rushed funeral with a dozen shellshocked attendees and move on as quickly as possible. No sharing of happy memories; no celebration of life.

Suicide kills twice. It kills the person you love, and then it kills the entire life they led.

Because no one will talk about them.

If someone you loved committed suicide, I want to just let you know that if you want, you can skip this chapter.

We're going to talk about it, and it might be painful. Skip ahead if you're not in a place where you want to do that. (But you know what? If you're anything like me, I bet you're *eager* to talk about it. Because no one else will.)

So, yes—the worst thing I ever went through was the suicide of my nephew, Cole. He was thirteen, my sister's child, and he'd been living with us on and off. He was a beautiful kid, a sweet boy who was as much a son to me and Brian as either of our own.

He was a kid who, like so many other kids, made some mistakes that led to more mistakes. Those mistakes led to rehab. And he never made it out.

When someone takes their own life, the questions come hard and fast at first, like everyone is absolutely desperate to find the responsible party. *Did you know? Why didn't he say anything? Who was with him? Did you notice any signs? Why would he do this? Did he leave a note?*

My only answer, in those first gut-wrenching days after his passing, when I could barely get out of bed, let alone engage in any kind of morbid detective work to solve the "mystery" of his suicide:

Who the fuck cares?

He was gone, and figuring out the *why* of it all wasn't going to bring him back.

Then there was the fact that there *was* no mystery. It was pretty fucking clear what had happened. He'd been sent to rehab instead of juvie, after going up in front of the same judge for petty crimes like vandalism and marijuana possession one too many times. He was depressed and anxious. He got put on suicide watch almost right away.

But the weeks went by, and he got through it, day by day. He got better.

There was just one problem: he'd thought he was in rehab *instead of* juvie. He didn't realize that he still had to go there after he was done with his program. And the night before he was supposed to be done with his time there, when he thought he was finally coming home the next day, one of the staff at the rehab center casually mentioned that he wasn't going home, he was going to jail.

Nobody knows why he was left alone for forty-five minutes to take a shower (suicide watch means *watch*, after all), but he was. That was all the time he needed.

The insane unfairness of it still chokes me to this day like a hand around my throat. Like a punch straight in the middle of my stomach. *He was left alone. Why the fuck would you leave him alone?*

That's how life is—that's how cruel it can get. Some stranger in a rehab center can make a shitty decision against regulations, go outside to smoke or look at their Snapchat, and just like that, so many lives are destroyed.

When Cole died, I was obliterated. I've said it before, and I'll say it again: it was worse than when we lost Jakob. The day I learned that he had committed suicide my world stopped for a number of days. I have no memory, I don't remember where I walked, I don't remember what I said, I don't remember who I saw.

It was like the earth dropped out from under my feet and I was falling, flailing, into a black pit of grief. There was nothing to stop the rage and devastation and crippling sense of unfairness, nothing that could be done to help the situation. It was just all-encompassing darkness.

And silence.

I'd been through it with Jakob—I'd been in the shit. I'd gotten all the silver linings, the "heroes" lining up to tell me what I hadn't tried yet to fix myself. I'd gone back into the darkness with Jax's birth and time in the NICU, and had the mental scars to prove it—and the bruises deep in my soul from the unrelenting judgment and shaming coming at me from all sides.

So when Cole died, I braced myself.

But there was nothing.

No one said anything. No one called. No one offered advice. No one mentioned him again.

It was like he just disappeared. Like he was erased.

And that was somehow worse than every well-intentioned word I'd ever heard.

THE ONLY ONE TO SPEAK

I had an anxiety attack in the parking lot outside Cole's funeral. I could barely stand; my legs wouldn't work. My cousin had to practically carry me in.

Inside, there were his school counselors, past teachers, friends, other family. All sitting silently. There was no body; it was just a big room where a bunch of people had gathered to sit not saying anything. I barely heard the service as it was delivered.

The silence was deafening. Why wasn't anyone talking about him? Had the manner in which he'd left us disqualified him from any kind of remembrance? Was it easier for everyone to just pretend he hadn't existed?

I couldn't stand it, so when it was time, I stood. I needed someone to break the silence. I needed someone to say something about the beautiful boy who had been like a son to me.

I took a deep breath and started talking. "I just need everyone to know who Cole was," I said. "He was the kid who always said *I love you*. No matter how mad he was, he'd always say it. We need to remember that. He was emotionally so full of love that he would never not say it. And yeah, he was disappointed in life, and it was a struggle for him to get through the next five minutes. We can talk about the fact that he committed suicide. We can talk about how he didn't leave a note. We can talk about how we'll never really know the whole story of what was going on inside him, how all the help we gave him still wasn't enough."

People were nodding, but many looked uncomfortable.

I'd said the "s" word. I'd acknowledged what we were all doing there.

"We can talk about how he died, and we can also talk about the boy he was before those last five minutes. He loved Batman blankets and burgers. He said simple is always better. He was young and finding his way, loved his family all in specific special ways, loved dogs, camping, fishing, Halloween. He was the light of my life. No matter what, he still looked at me and had that light in his eyes and all those things could have been different now, but they aren't. Although he thought he could change the world by leaving it, he was wrong! He was a boy that committed suicide. But that doesn't change who he was."

For several minutes, I was able to hold it together enough to talk about Cole. I needed to make sure everyone remembered him correctly. I couldn't stand the thought that he would be gone forever and no one would say anything. I couldn't stand the idea that he could be wiped from this world and also wiped from our memories.

CHAPTER FIVE

THE SILENT LOSS

I was recently talking to a friend who lost her brother to suicide, and she said something that resonated hard.

"I can talk about my mom's cancer all day. And I can cry about it all day. But I never talk about my brother's suicide, and I've never cried for him."

Even alone with her thoughts, she kept them locked away.

Why do we do that?

In all the ways that matter, suicide is just like any other death. There's an added layer of *what the fuck* and *how did I not see* and that detective work I mentioned earlier, everyone trying to figure out who's to blame (because if it's someone's fault, it's less likely to happen to them; but if it's just a random, unpredictable event, there's no way to control and therefore prevent it).

But all of the grieving, the physical debilitation, the emotional devastation... it's all the same. So why do we treat it

"From my experience as a once young daughter in college whose mother was battling cancer years ago, I watched as my mother's friends didn't know what to say, so they just stayed silent. I guess they didn't want to bring up the actual "c" word. My mother needed to talk and share her feelings about this battle. I did my best to hold space for her, not commenting, just listening. Working as a therapist over the past twenty-five years, I continue to hold space for others who are in challenging phases of their life and often ask, "do you just want me to listen, or are you open to talking about things?" Often, the answer is both.

Fast forward to 2016 when my brother unexpectedly took his life, and a year later, I was in a hair salon feeling trapped in the chair as the salon owner and her client were talking about a mutual acquaintance who had recently taken their life. Neither seemed to know this poor soul well and I became flooded with emotions. When I gently shared what i was experiencing, they looked at me and said, "oh, we didn't know." Then, they proceeded to quietly talk even more about suicide, expressing their anger and ill-informed opinions on the subject. Needless to say, I left and never went back. I later found out my hairstylist quit; I envision it was in a stand for me (wishful thinking). My wish is that people don't stay silent but become aware that at any moment, you can be within earshot of someone who is suffering. Being able to attune to who is around you before you say that fucked-up thing is important."

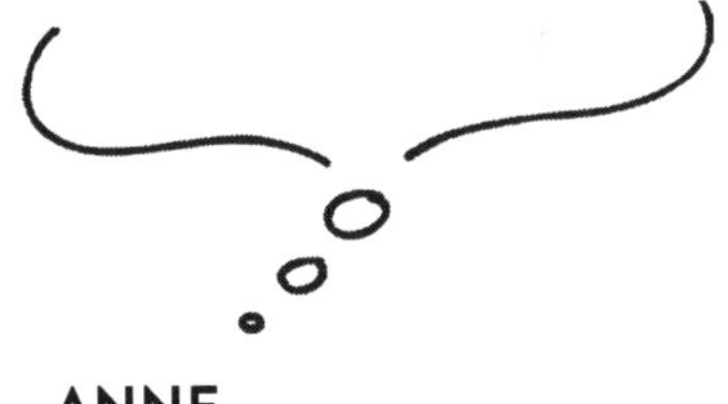

ANNE

like we're not allowed to talk about mourning? Why do we put suicide away in a box inside our minds?

The longer the silence and the harder the silence, the more guilt the left behind person is feeling. Suicide is a death where other people are the victim. They become the victim from the wound that is opened up. The guilt is so intense, so all encompassing—and it's all that's left, because we don't have the whole story. We need the whole story, and we'll never know it. So we insert ourselves. We fill in the blanks. With ourselves. With everything we didn't do.

The reason I can talk about suicide? I don't insert myself into Cole's story. I don't talk about his story like it's mine, because it's not. I have zero guilt. It was his story, his choice. There's nothing I can do. Guilting myself, and being quiet and letting the guilt build into bitterness and toxicity and disease (guilt over Cole will be the death of both my parents), I live. I move through life with the pain, like a backpack I'm wearing at all times.

How did I live through it? I put on the pain backpack and I got stronger. I gave back to other people. I worked with young kids, training them in the gym to build their physical and emotional confidence. I worked early on with a young girl whose mom was terrified—her daughter was being bullied, and she was worried about the impact. Cole had been bullied. I got certified in Youth Fitness and Performance and took the girl in, worked with her, built up her confidence. Cole had always felt so much better when we worked out together. I tried to help kids rather than letting my mind fill in the gaps with guilt.

My theory is that it's impossible for healthy people to understand how someone could take their own life, so their brains just freeze in panic when they're confronted with it. They literally don't know what to say. They just know they don't want to talk about the big, scary, unpredictable, uncontrollable, deadly elephant in the room that could also come for someone they love at any moment.

By the way, if anyone *for sure* wants to get punched by me, say that suicide is selfish. (Remember when I said I wasn't violent? I lied.)

How do you know it was selfish? How do you know what they thought? Why the fuck would you make their choice about you? How dare you center yourself in their choice?

If you take one thing and one thing only away from this book: do not *ever* say that. EVER. DON'T FUCKING SAY THAT. Even if you're talking to a friend about someone else, don't let that come out of your mouth. It's never okay.

Suicide takes the one life, and leaves many lives in shambles. Suicide leaves questions and doubt, sorrow and sadness that not even over time gets better, acceptance that not even over time is understood. Suicide doesn't offer explanations because it's forever. It's forever; the human is gone. There's no opportunity to ask questions or solve the problems.

Talking to others who have lost loved ones to suicide, it's clear that there is so much we can be doing to support each other. There are so many stories we can trade; we might be in the world's saddest club that nobody else wants to find themselves in, but at least we have a lot in common to talk about.

So let's talk about it.

If you know someone who's going through a suicide, *talk to them.* Talk about their loved one, the same way you would if they'd died any other way. Ask them about their loved one's favorite movies and food and music. Ask them what their most cherished memory is. Help bring the person back to life by celebrating the person they were, regardless of how they died.

Because it's not fair that we lose them twice.

REAL SUPPORT VS. THE PERFORMANCE

I lied before—when Cole died, it wasn't *complete* silence.

I did get one "at least".

At least he was just your nephew, not your son or anything.

Inside, I boiled when I heard this. I wanted to fire back:

"Holy cow, Charlotte, are you fucking kidding me with that? I can't even summon a sarcastic response. That sucked. Don't say things like that."

And you know what? Unlike other times when I bit my tongue, trying not to upset the other person, this time, I did what was best for me in that moment. I *did* fire back with that.

Cole's death was officially the turning point for me in a lifetime of getting firebombed by well-intentioned words. It was the exact moment my very last fuck ran out.

It was like I came awake afterward with a certain clarity. I was tired of the well-intentioned words, and I was tired of the silence around suicide. I was positively exhausted by constantly having to look out for *other people's* feelings when I was the one who needed support. And I was tired of handholding people who didn't know what support looked like.

This was when I stopped worrying about hurting people's feelings, and started worrying more about the people being hurt by their well-intentioned words.

I was tired of the performance of support. I decided it was time I start educating people on what real support was.

That's when the idea for this book was born.

WHY IS GOD SO **OBSESSED** WITH TESTING WHAT I CAN HANDLE? MAYBE HE COULD TURN HIS **FOCUS** INSTEAD TO, I DON'T KNOW, **WORLD HUNGER**, OR MASS SHOOTINGS, OR **CANCER**?

CH*PTER SIX

THANKS A LOT, GOD

I can't state this strongly enough:

Everything does NOT happen for a reason.

If you're offended, if you think I'm being insensitive to your religion, this chapter probably isn't for you. (And if you're using your religion as an excuse to be shitty to people, delete my number.)

Of all the well-intentioned words we're going to cover in this book, this one takes the cake.

"Everything happens for a reason."

"God has a plan."

"It was meant to be."

This one comes in various flavors, but the meaning is the same: *shut up and take the punches God is throwing at you, miserable human. Stop complaining.*

I don't know if this is actually comforting for religious people—I guess it must be, because they sure say it a lot.

I'm not religious (at least not in the pre-packaged, church-ready way people usually think of), so to me, it's practically an insult.

Oh, really? Your god thought it would be just an absolute hoot to kill my first child, then put me through hell with my second, and then just for a banger of an encore, kill my surrogate son?

Was he bored? Had he binge-watched everything on Netflix the night he made that "plan", or what?

"God doesn't give you anything you can't handle."

I mean, I guess I'm *flattered* that he thinks I can handle all this, but like, can I opt out, please?!

Why is God so obsessed with testing what I can handle? Maybe he could turn his focus instead to, I don't know, world hunger, or mass shootings, or cancer?

That's right. Cancer. Here's a thought, God: how about instead of testing people with cancer, you just get rid of it altogether?

This was my kneejerk reaction in the days, weeks, and months after the next *hilarious* punch in the gut life dealt me: being diagnosed with breast cancer.

(You thought after the death of two kids, a stint in the

NICU, and raging PTSD, things were about to look up in this story, didn't you? Surprise, bitches!)

When I got diagnosed with cancer, people were *really* adamant that God had something to do with it. That he had some master plan that involved me going through chemotherapy and radiation, getting a double mastectomy, and losing all my hair while trying to be a mom and run a business. And they came up and told me about that plan. A lot.

My response?

I'm not interested in the "plan" of any god that would give me cancer. Or give little kids cancer. Or give anyone cancer. Not super interested in what that asshole has to say, to be honest.

If God has a plan, then I guess it also involves me writing this book so I can tell the world to *please* stop bringing him up to people who are going through tough times.

CHAPTER SIX

LET ME OFF THIS ROLLERCOASTER

The PTSD that had taken root in the aftermath of Jax's birth came roaring back in the wake of Cole's suicide.

Once again, I don't have a whole lot of memories from that six-month period, except that I was in such a tailspin, such a shell of a person, that even my normally stable-as-a-rock relationship with Brian was hitting speedbumps. I knew I needed to pull myself out of the death spiral if I was going to come back to myself and be the wife and mom I'd imagined myself to be before my world had been blown apart.

You wouldn't think that bodybuilding could save a person, but for me, it really did. I needed a goal, and at 40, after two pregnancies, the idea of pushing and honing my body into competition-ready form seemed like the kind of Everest that would demand all the effort I had to give (and, conveniently, keep my mind and body occupied enough that the darkness had no room to leak into my world anymore).

At first, I got into it just for that reason: *this is the hardest thing I could pick to do, so let's do it.*

I stayed with it because, truly unexpectedly, it was one of the best forms of self-love I could have asked for. Spending day after day connecting with my body, listening to it, researching and planning the best meals to nourish it, and just focusing on *me* in the gym allowed me to simply... spend time with myself. Build back the Mell that had been broken down by so many proverbial kicks in the gut. I re-met myself during that training period, reacquainted myself with the optimistic, happy woman who had been so excited to first be pregnant with Jakob so many years ago.

This is not to say that nobody said shit to me during that time—oh man, did I catch a *lot* of shit. It wasn't well-intentioned, either. This was straight up passive-aggressive Karening of my every move. People—almost all women, much to my dismay (don't we have a sisterhood?! Aren't we supposed to be out here supporting each other?!)—couldn't drop enough hints about what they thought of my bodybuilding journey.

Everything from, "I *wish* I had so much time to spend in the gym. My kids take all of it up, though"—oh, gotcha, I'm a shitty selfish mom because I'm in self-love mode and daring to spend time on myself, instead of on taking care of other people. Heard.

To, "Well, we can't go to [insert restaurant] to eat because you know Mell's not going to be able to eat anything there." Does the actual meal I ingest when we go out really affect you all that much, Charlotte? I'll be fine. Yes, I'm paying a lot of attention to what I eat right now. No, I'm not suggesting you're deficient in some way for not doing the same.

It was like the women in my life, the fellow wives and moms, were shocked and betrayed that I *dared* to think about myself for the first time in years. "Think about your-self?! But what about *all the other people* who are more important than you?!" seemed to be their general POV, and more than anything, it just made me sad.

Growing up a girl and then living as a woman in our society, it's impossible not to notice that we're expected to put ourselves last and take care of everyone else first. I know a woman who once joked, "When they tell me to put my own oxygen mask on first in the airplane, that's the closest to self-care I get."

So yeah, of course I'd always felt the weight of those expectations. But to see those expectations acted out so plainly by all the women I knew—to hear them repeating the language of that unfair burden, and shaming me every step of the way for shrugging off those expectations in favor of my own goals—felt like a betrayal. It was disappointing. And it was sad. It felt like a projection; these women were projecting their own lack of permission to self-love.

Listen to me, and really hear this: *you do not need anyone's permission to love yourself.*

No matter how much people try to make you think you need their permission, you don't. You're allowed to love yourself as much as you want. Even if that means time away from your kids. Even if that means time away from taking care of every single person in your orbit.

What you want and how you feel matter. And you get to

spend time on those things.

I got the judging and shaming from all sides during my bodybuilding training... and it was loud.

Luckily, though, I had just been through several years of loss, death, and bodily harm, so I had just about the thickest skin imaginable! Oh, you want to shame me for going to the gym? I've literally buried two kids in 5 years. Come at me.

At 40, I did my first bodybuilding competition. It was weird and wonderful. I felt like myself again—someone who had goals, who worked on herself, who went after passions just because she wanted them, not because she was obligated to. I was pumped to set an example for Jax: *in this family, we love our bodies, and we love ourselves, and we deserve the time and space to go after our dreams.*

At the same time I was rebuilding my relationship with my body (which, can we stand and do a slow clap for my body? Holy shit, what it went through in such a short period of time, and how it bounced back, is something I'll always be in awe of), I was deepening my relationship with the women I coached at Her Well Wisher. I'd added a few certifications to my personal training arsenal: prenatal, postnatal, special populations.

Training a clientele that was mostly women exposed me to just about all the well-intentioned words you can think of, like secondhand smoke. Women would come into the gym depressed or reeling from some crazy word-bomb that had been dropped on them. We'd all commiserate, laugh it off together, sweat it out and let it go. Physical exertion is a pretty effective form of therapy when you need to shake off some of the everyday trauma, the little moment-to-moment jabs, that come with being a woman.

In the years after Jakob's death, Jax's birth, and Cole's passing, I came back to myself and rebuilt into the person I wanted to be. I was confident. I was happy. I was satisfied.

And then cancer came along and fucked me right up.

CHAPTER SIX

EVERY WELL-INTENTIONED WORD EVER

If you're having trouble believing that people actually say some of the stuff I've written about in this book, getting cancer would convince you in a split second. (But don't. I really don't recommend cancer. Way better ways to spend your time.)

Cancer is one of those things that cuts across all the social constructs we have: class, race, gender, religion. It affects everyone equally. Like the DMV. No matter who you are, you have to, at some point, drag your ass down to the DMV and get in line with the rest of the world. Cancer is the DMV of the health world; sure some people might be predisposed to going to the DMV more often because they move a lot or have a tendency to lose their wallet, but at the end of the day, *everyone* has the same chance of getting stuck in a long line there, and no one is safe.

When I got cancer, I got lucky in a few ways. Number one, we caught it early. It had been living rent-free in my body for just nine months by the time it was detected, and originally, it was diagnosed as a cyst (rudest bait and switch of all time, if you ask me). When I was officially diagnosed with breast cancer, it was Stage 1.

And boy, did everyone have something to say about that.

"Thank God it's only stage 1, you're going to be fine."

First off, I'm not thanking God for shit, since supposedly he's the one who did this to me. And second, stage 1 is still CANCER. You know, cancer, the Big C, the thing that progresses from stage 1 to 2 to 3 to 4 to an early coffin? I'd prefer stage zero, stage nonexistent, thank you very much.

"Stage 1 is a breeze, my sister had it and she didn't even lose her hair."

Yeah, this is practically a Cancun vacation! Chemo and radiation, margaritas on the beach, same thing, right? (Also, I *did* lose my hair, so... what do you know, cancer is different for everyone!)

"Stage 1 is the good kind, you're strong, you've got this!"

No, actually, I don't got this, cancer is fucking scary.

Here's the thing about stage 1 cancer.

It's still cancer.

Was I immediately about to die? No, not likely (unless it was choking on my own tongue from biting it when people lobbed their well-intentioned words at me).

Was I still going to go through the whole drama—chemo, radiation, double mastectomy? Yup. The whole enchilada. Stage 1, Stage 4, it's all cancer, and the treatment is the same: poison *it* before it can poison *you* to death, and also cut it right off if at all possible.

So, if someone you know gets diagnosed with stage 1 cancer, and you breathe a big sigh of relief in front of them and get ready to tell them how it's totally no big deal, stage 1 is child's play, they got lucky?

Don't fucking say that. Trust me.

Cancer turns your entire life upside down, no matter what

stage you're in.

When I started moving through the new reality I found myself in after cancer suddenly blew in like a storm and turned my technicolor life into shades of black and gray, I found myself running up against more well-intentioned words than I ever had before. People just couldn't stop saying things that made me cringe, that made me angry, that made me want to crawl into bed and never come out.

When you've been through multiple tragedies, there comes a point when you see human behavior not as you *wish* it to be, but as it actually is.

People aren't what you hope they are. People are just people. They're going to act in self-interest, they're going to project their own fears onto you, and even while they genuinely love and want to support you, they're going to hurt your feelings badly.

I had to make a choice in those days: should I give up on people entirely and turn into a cynical, hollow, bitter woman, someone who wallowed in misfortune and spent all her free time bitching about the terrible things people said to her?

Or should I find a way to let their well-intentioned words slide off me like rainwater off a roof?

I already had one kind of cancer eating away at me on the inside. I didn't want the well-intentioned words I kept hearing to worm their way into my soul and poison me as well. Chemo and radiation were already bombarding my body with toxicity (but the good kind, the kind that kills cancer—thanks, chemo and radiation!) and I didn't have an inch of space left for any more.

So I decided to change my mindset. This was when my well-wisher project really took on primary significance in my life.

Wishing someone well *before* reacting like their word bomb had just exploded in my face took the sting out of what they'd said. Instead of throwing up a wall to shield me from their grenades, I put up a lens to change how I saw each person. The lens was optimism, compassion, understanding, and wishing them well.

I chose to look at them and wish them well before responding to what they'd say. After all, I had no idea what they were carrying; I had no way of knowing what fears and life experiences had brought them to a place where they were literally expressing relief and calling me "lucky" for having the kind of cancer I had.

The well-wish stopped all my judgment. It was like their well-intentioned words bounced off my well-wishing lens and scattered to the wind where it couldn't hurt me.

Did this mean I *never* responded, though?

No way. Sometimes people said things *so* wild, so completely outrageous, that I felt a duty to save the next cancer patient they'd run into from a similar grenade.

And in a surprise to absolutely no one who knows how women are treated in our society, the *worst* things I heard were about my appearance.

CHAPTER SIX

YOU'RE SO VAIN

First: I hate the concept of vanity.

I know it's a bible thing, one of the seven deadly sins, and that's why the concept is so rooted in our minds as a "bad" thing.

But since when is it a bad thing to want to look good, and to love how you look?

Even more, since when is it not allowed to say you *don't* like how you look, and you wish you could change it?

It's not vain for women to take comfort and pleasure in the beautiful, feminine parts of us. Our hair, our breasts, our skin, our energy and vitality. I *loved* having beautiful, long blonde hair. I loved styling it and the way it framed my face. I loved how I could change my hair and take on a whole different energy just by putting it up or wearing it down. It made me feel beautiful, sexy, like myself. A lot of my identity was wrapped up in my hair, and I don't even think that's uncommon or abnormal.

When I lost my hair, and *no one* would give me the space to feel bad about it, it was tough.

Having short hair hurt more than if I'd been totally bald. It wasn't just a different hairstyle; it was like looking at a stranger in the mirror. So much of my feeling of self-recognition, of *knowing* myself, came from seeing the swing of that long blonde ponytail ("ponytail power" was something I'd say to hype us all up during workouts) in the mirror, or catching a glimpse of it in the glass of a store window when walking by.

Being sad about it, though? Apparently that wasn't allowed.

"It's just hair. It'll grow back in no time."

Great. I'll just shut up for the whole two to three years it will take to grow this back to the length I had before. (Also, it's *not* just hair, it's *me*, don't you get that?)

"Good thing you have a beautiful face; you can rock short hair."

So you're saying that my face cancels out my hair? Because my short hair is... what? Ugly? What if I *didn't* have a beautiful face? What then?

"At least it takes less time to do your hair now, right?"

Anyone who's had short hair is laughing. Actually, *no*, it takes way more time and requires three different products to make it look good. Before, I used to just comb out my hair, put it up in a bun, and have flowing princess waves when I took it back down.

"It's fine, they make great wigs."

Holy shit! Exciting news, everybody! It's fine! Charlotte says it's *fine!* We can all stop feeling bad now, because Charlotte saw some movie where the long-suffering cancer patient comes out in a wig and everyone claps and the music tells us she's going to be fine because she's not bald anymore!

"What does Brian think about your short hair?"

I have to admit that this one just made me laugh. First,

yes, of *course* I'm looking at being robbed of my health and identity by a vicious disease through the lens of whether a man still thinks I'm attractive. Second, if you know Brian, you'd know that's the stupidest question you could ever ask. What does Brian think? Brian's glad his wife is alive, and that's pretty much all-encompassing at the moment.

When I was bald, I rocked my bald head. I didn't wear a wig—no shade to anyone who does, it just wasn't for me. I found it easier to go through what was happening to me without pretending it wasn't. I've always been a confronter; when reality rears its ugly head, I like to run up and challenge it to a fight, not ignore it and pretend it'll go away.

But was I insecure? Sure. And it's not vain to say so. We're allowed to take pride in our beauty. We're allowed to have our looks be a piece of our identity. There's nothing wrong with that, and I hate that we've been made to believe that there is by centuries of being told we're vain for caring about how we look.

The volume got turned up on my insecurity when I decided I wasn't going to mess around with "what if" and opted for a double mastectomy to completely remove the chance of any cancer sticking around.

Because if you think your hair is part of your identity as a woman, *wow* is that even more true for your boobs.

The well-intentioned words that kicked off this book were truly some of the most stinging I've ever heard.

"At least you got a boob job out of the deal!"

Holy. Shit. Are you kidding me? (First off, been there, done that. These boobs were fresh, and only like five years old! I would've liked more mileage out of them.) I'm literally having surgery to remove body parts. Parts that have been with me since I first became a woman. Parts that fed and gave life to my son. Parts that have defined every outfit I've ever worn, that have made me immediately recognizable as a feminine being.

Why on earth would I be celebrating replacing them?

There's an insidious undertone to those well-intentioned

words. It's implying that women should *want* boob jobs, that our natural bodies aren't good enough. That we should do a happy dance when disease hits us because we get to swap out inferior parts for brand new, better ones.

It's like that line from *The Devil Wears Prada:* "I'm one stomach flu away from my goal weight!"

That's the vanity women are allowed to have in our culture. We're allowed to pursue beauty as long as we're suffering to do it. We're allowed to want to look our best as long as "best" is approved and sold to us, not naturally come by.

Because get this: when I actually wanted a boob job, all I heard was, "No, you don't need that, you're beautiful as is, don't do that!" But when it was time to have a mastectomy to save my life? Suddenly I heard was, "Hallelujah, you're getting a boob job!" So we just get to constantly make up new rules about when it's acceptable to want a boob job, is that it?

As a woman, you're never allowed to be unhappy with your current circumstance. You always have to find a way to be good with it. An Unhappy Woman is the worst thing you can be in our society. You're not allowed to want things to be different—even if you have cancer.

The whole experience was eye-opening. Having cancer, in a strange way, made me clearer than ever on my connection with my womanhood—because it felt like it was constantly under assault.

You know what *was* great to hear about my appearance, though?

"I love your hair; you look like P!nk!"

Well, I love her, she's amazing and beautiful, so *thank you!*

"Your skin is glowing, you look radiant!"

Thanks, I've been sleeping like fifteen hours a day, because I can't move, and it's one of the only things I have going for me right now.

Or even just something as simple as, "You look great."

"Looking back now to the beginning of my cancer journey, everyone seemed more interested in learning what the doctors told me or concerned or asked about my diagnosis versus how I was actually dealing with it, or how I was doing mentally. Even though I always say I don't want to show my vulnerability, in hindsight, that may have been the key to having a smoother journey, avoiding the extreme highs and lows of the emotional rollercoaster.

However, I couldn't be vulnerable, because no one gave me the opportunity. No one asked. No one came to visit me and be there in person and by my side through this journey. I eventually broke and boy did it come flooding out.

But I get it now. I went through a life altering event. I

cried to know that I did the same thing to a friend who's husband went through cancer. I cried because I was not there for them. I stupidly thought they would want to keep to themselves and was scared I might say the wrong thing, so I didn't even try to be there for them.

I am no longer the person I was before. I've lost a bit of myself, my being, my existence. I'm medically induced menopausal which makes me feel less of a woman. My right breast is smaller. I have scars and thinning hair.

But I have the drive to move on and learn to embrace my new norm."

AMY

It seems like it pales in comparison to the rest of what we're going through, but just hearing a simple compliment sometimes makes all the difference.

After all, if I have to have cancer, it's nice to at least feel pretty.

YOU DON'T KNOW WHAT I CAN HANDLE, AND NEITHER DOES GOD

Remember how I said before that I put my well-wisher lens in place, and used it as a focusing element to deflect people's toxic well-intentioned words away from me?

And that I wished them well before reacting in anger, frustration, or any of the other dozen things I was feeling as a result of those well-intentioned words?

Well, there was one flavor of well-intentioned words that didn't get my compassion. Or understanding. Or even my well wishes.

And that's... all the God stuff.

"God doesn't give you anything you can't handle."

What on earth does that even mean?

First off, are you saying God gave me cancer? Because if so, he can fuck off.

Second, what about people who get cancer and die? Was it because God gave them something they *couldn't* handle?

Were they just not strong enough? Not brave enough?

If I die, does that prove you (and God) wrong?

I truly don't care what you believe—I think you should believe whatever you want, whatever works for you. I'm not judging anyone's religion, and I would stand up and fight for their right to practice it however they want.

But do you honestly not see how absolutely deranged it is to go up to a sick person and tell them that your god gave them their cancer on purpose to test their mettle?

It's fucking *wild.*

"Everything happens for a reason."

Please, *please* explain the reasons that my sons died and my baby lived in an incubator for three months and I had a mental breakdown and then got cancer. Please explain the master plan behind that. Because honestly? I feel like if my life were a movie, I'd walk out of the theater saying it was overdramatic, chaotic, and not super believable. Nobody loses two kids *and then gets cancer* in the movies. It's insane.

There's no plan.

That's the truth. This is all one messy, fly-by-the-seat-of-our-pants rollercoaster speeding steadily towards our inevitable demise. There's no grand vision. There's no person sitting up in the sky ticking off a list, going, "Oh, right on schedule, there's Mell's cancer diagnosis. Wow, I knew the new hair would look good on her!"

The messiness of our lives, the chaos and unpredictability and sometimes insanity of our circumstances, is actually one of the best things about it.

I *really* don't love that the mess gave me cancer, but hey, I've been through some shit. I know the drill.

I want to move through life not anticipating what comes next, or wondering what new blow God has to deal me after I'm done dealing with this one. I want to take what comes at me supported by the people who love me, just because they love me, not because "I can handle it" or "there's a reason."

Sometimes, there is no reason. Things happen, and they're terrible. And there's no explanation.

All we can do is hold each other close on the ride and make sure we get to the end in one piece.

I find that the most comforting of all—I don't have to rely on God's (batshit crazy) plan to save me.

Real support is knowing that we only have each other, and that's more than enough.

WHAT WOULD IT LOOK LIKE TO JUST **WALK** YOUR PATH AND **ACCEPT** WHAT IT HOLDS, NO MATTER HOW **PAINFUL?**

CH*PTER SEVEN

WOULD'VE, COULD'VE, SHOULD'VE

At this point in the book, we've gone through all the major categories of well-intentioned words. Let's recap.

1. "At least..." Don't fucking say that.

2. "The silver lining is..." *Really* don't fucking say that.

3. Don't be the shame police; wish her well instead.

4. "Have you tried..." Did you really just fucking say that?

5. Silence is not golden. Let's stop erasing suicide.

6. "Everything happens for a reason..." ...including me never speaking to you again.

And while I'll repeat for the tenth time that authenticity has to come from you, and I can't tell you what to say, let's also recap some of the things I *loved* to hear when I was going through any of the all-time worst moments of my life.

1. "I love you."

2. "I'm here for you."

3. "Can I help you with [insert item]?"

4. "What do you need right now?"

5. "You look great."

6. "What was he like?"

7. "This sucks. I'm here."

8. "You're brave."

"She said *what?!*" (Okay, this one we didn't recap, but trust me, validating a friend who's asking if they're crazy to be upset over some well-intentioned words can be the best support they could ask for.)

This chapter is a grab bag of sorts, because there are a bunch of commonly heard well-intentioned words that don't really fall into any one category. They're brought together only by one unifying thread:

They're not actually about *you*. They're about the well-intentioned person.

You know when you can tell someone is pretending to talk about you, but actually just talking about themselves? Everyone's experienced this at some point: that one person who turns everything you say into a story about themselves. You're trying to spill your guts about something shitty going down in your life, and their only response is, "Well, when *I* got laid off, I was on LinkedIn the very next day so I didn't waste any time."

Awesome, glad to hear it, but we were actually talking about *me*. Or at least, I thought we were. I'm not sure what you thought.

People who can't conceive of life in any other way than through their own lens are more common than you'd imagine. And we talked about why earlier in the book: it's natural to immediately try to relate through your own experiences, because after all, it's all you know.

The problem arises when that's the *only* way you can relate. When the only response you have to someone expressing their own pain is to tell them about yours.

Think about it in terms of regular everyday stuff, not disease, death, and tragedy:

You run into a coworker in the hall of your office, and they look a little pale. "Ugh," they say. "I think I'm coming down with something. I feel like shit."

"I had a cold once," you respond, then walk off, proud of the nice moment you just shared.

Or you're at lunch with a friend and they're talking about financial dire straits. "I'm just not sure what we're going to do," they say. "I'm worried we're going to lose the house."

"Mmm-hmm," you say comfortingly. "We had a hefty property tax bill last year."

See how odd and off-putting that is? You'd never do that in conversation, because it's antisocial and you'd have no friends.

So then why do people do it in reaction to tragedy?

You tell someone a loved one has passed away, and their response is about *their* loved one who passed away. You share that you're going through health problems, and suddenly you're hearing all about their chronic IBS.

Or the worst form of this, and the one you *really* do not want to fucking say:

The dreaded "should". (Or, as I call it, should-ing all over me.)

"Should" is a cousin of "Have you tried", but it's worse. That they're not *implying* you haven't done enough or did something wrong, they're outright *saying* it.

"You should get out of the house. You should take walks around the neighborhood. You need to start feeling better."

Oh wow, Charlotte, sorry, I didn't know I was messing up your incredibly tight schedule that is, for some reason, tied to my processing of grief.

"You should check out [insert internet cancer remedy or snake oil salesman]. It saved my mom's life."

Your mom was also doing chemo, so I think it's more probable the chemo saved her life, and not whatever "viral smoothie doctors DON'T want you to know about" you saw on Instagram, but okay.

"You should take it easy on the workouts, I had separated abs after pregnancy and I..."

This isn't about you! And I didn't ask!

People were should-ing all over me in the wake of each of the personal tragedies I endured over the past several years, and it really came to a fever pitch during my cancer journey. It's amazing all the ways people have of telling you that you're doing cancer wrong.

Why are we so obsessed with making someone else's story all about *us?*

THERE'S NO ROI ON SUPPORT

We live in a transactional culture (thanks, capitalism!) where if anyone is going to expend a resource—money, time, energy, emotional support—they've been conditioned to expect something in return.

We're trained to think in terms of profit. What am I getting out of this? What do I have now that I didn't have before?

The problem with this is what we talked about earlier: real support has no ROI.

Because ROI is about *you*. What *you* get. And support is about *them*.

True support completely decenters you in favor of centering the person needing it. You're not going to get anything out of it, and that's what makes it support.

Sure, you'll feel good knowing you supported someone you love, and that hopefully you made them feel better for a little while—but if that's *why* you're doing it, stop. Examine why you feel the need for a reward at all.

Why do so many of us feel the need to get paid for doing something that should be free—and not just free, but the table stakes of any healthy relationship?

I find that when it comes to information, people generally break down into two main types (again, if vast overgeneralizations make you uncomfortable, just skip ahead):

1. **People who watch the news:** These people *need to know* every little detail about what's going on with other people. Knowing things makes them feel powerful and special. They'll get the tea, they'll pour the tea, they'll even make the tea if it means they get to talk about other people's lives.

2. **People who don't watch the news:** These people not only don't need to know, they don't *want* to know. This could be for multiple reasons: they have enough going on in their own lives that they don't need to be in other people's business, or maybe they get uncomfortable talking about people who aren't in the room, or maybe they just really value privacy. In any case, they're not looking for the tea and don't really want to be involved.

When it comes to supporting someone who's going through a tough time, you might think that Person 1 is going to be a better support; they're engaged, they care enough to get the details, and they're sure as hell going to be listening to what you say (because they need to memorize it so they can spend that information currency when they're out at drinks and recounting your story for other people).

Person 2 is actually going to be your ride or die here. Why? Because Person 2 isn't in it for a payday. They're not there for you so they can soak up the details; in fact, they don't want or need the details at all. They're not going to be the ones asking, when your nephew commits suicide, "Did he leave a note?" or "How did he do it?" or "Who found him?" or "Was he on medication?" (Answers: No, None of your business, Why the fuck do you care, and What exactly are you implying?)

They're going to just put their arms around you and keep you from flying apart at the seams.

For *nothing* in return.

Person 1, on the other hand, is going to *seem* supportive, but eventually they're going to drop a "should". They're going to bring your situation back around to themselves.

Because that's what it's been about the entire time.

Why?

Why can't you just let it be my tragedy?

It's an odd thing to feel upstaged in your own tough time—because after all, we don't *want* to be going through it. I'd have given anything to have Jakob and Cole back. I'd have moved heaven and earth to have carried Jax to term. I didn't *want* to be grief-stricken, broken, moving through life like crawling through a cold mud pit.

But I was. And every time someone made my tragedy about *them*, I felt like mine didn't matter. I felt like *I* didn't matter.

True support doesn't need an ROI. What someone in the pain cave needs is to feel heard, validated, and held. They don't need to know how you tackled the same problem. They don't need to hear what they should have done instead.

"When I was first diagnosed with cancer, friends I did not even remember meeting suddenly came out of the woodwork. I was 28 years old, newly married, teaching elementary school, and otherwise healthy. The C word came as a complete and utter shock. Everyone offered unsolicited advice about their mother's brother's uncle who had cancer 25 years ago, what to eat, what not to eat, and so much more. I was scared, and didn't know what to make of all of these newfound friends trying to "help". I listened, quietly rolled my eyes, and plunged ahead. Until I received the greatest phone call of them all. It came from a family friend I had known for half of my life.

"Jaime, I do not know what to say to you. I cannot believe this is real. I know everyone is offering you support and love in the form of phone calls, meals, books, knitted socks, you name it. I can get you all of that too. But, what I'm offering is totally different. If you ever feel like you've hit a wall and just want to yell **FUCKETY FUCK FUCK FUCK** at the top of your lungs, I'm your girl! Call me day or night, and scream! I'm here for you."

The irony of this story is that now, almost 25 years since Maria offered this to me, her very own daughter is facing breast cancer. As soon as I heard, I called Maria and offered that right back to her. Things have come full circle!

JAIME

WOULD'VE, COULD'VE, SHOULD'VE

During the heartbreakingly brief but life-changing time I got to spend with Cole, I used to teach him something we still teach Jax to this day:

We don't use forever words.

Forever words are words that try to change reality. *I should have turned left instead of right. If I would have just done xyz, this would never have happened. I could have prevented it.*

We don't use those words in our family. No would've, could've, should've. It's not possible to change what happened, so why set up the premise that it is?

Despite all my best parenting wisdom thrown at the boys, there was a time when I lived inside those forever words. In the days after losing Jakob, I ran through every second of my pregnancy in my mind and found ways to stab myself in the heart over and over.

CHAPTER SEVEN

I should've gotten a checkup sooner.

Why the fuck did I eat tuna? I should have been eating cleaner.

I should have paid more attention to that cramping. I shouldn't have written it off as normal.

For a period of time, I was convinced that I had been the sole cause of Jakob's loss through my own selfish, stupid choices. This period of time didn't last long, thankfully; even out of my mind with grief, I knew that all I was doing was creating a villain to blame everything on so I could beat it to death with my bare hands. (Even if that villain was me.)

I also convinced myself that if I cataloged every move I'd made that had "led to" the loss of my son, I could hold myself superior to the past version of myself who had made those mistakes. I could become a woman who would *never* lose a baby again. I would know better. I would see disaster coming and jump out of the way.

It was a fantasy world, obviously, and one that was created

just to torture myself in. This wasn't processing grief; it was self-hating for the sake of wrestling back some shred of a sense of control.

It wasn't real, and it didn't last. I was left just as empty as I was the moment they took Jakob from my arms.

When we use forever words, all it does it create self-doubt and anxiety. It creates the feeling that the thing we fear or the bad thing that happened to us can actually be different, if we just think of the different course we *should have* taken. But why do that? We can't go back and actually take it, so why map out a different road that would have led us away from suffering and towards happiness?

It's a false reality. It doesn't exist. And all it does is make our suffering worse.

A "should've story", as I call it, builds a story that gives you a choice. In your mind, inside the should've story, you're staring at two doors. One is the door you originally went through. Did it *cause* the suffering you're currently experiencing? Maybe it did, maybe it didn't. It doesn't matter; it's what happened. The other door is fiction; it doesn't exist.

And yet, for a brief moment inside that should've story, it's real.

You *could* choose Door #2.

But you don't, not because it's in the past and physically impossible, but because... oh, insert all the vicious self-recriminations we beat ourselves up with. *If I'd been smarter. If I'd paid more attention. If I didn't have my head up my ass. If I'd only listened. If I weren't me. I'm the problem. I'm the one who picked Door #1, because I wasn't good enough. And look where that got me.*

While you're deep in this self-loathing spiral, life is happening, and you're not living it. In fact, you *can't* live it, because you're stuck living in the past, playing over and over the moment when you reached out and grabbed the cold doorknob of Door #1 like an absolute idiot and fucked up your whole life.

Why are you creating a reality in which you're doomed to fail? Why are you pretending there were two doors in the first place?

Here's the thing I need you to know, if you've ever lain awake at night with the image of Door #2 looming in front of you, your heart beating in time with the *would've, could've, should've* clanging around inside your brain, swallowing your grief and shame and regret at not choosing the right path that would have spared you all the pain:

It's not your fault. And you couldn't have done anything differently.

There are not two doors. At any given moment, there is only one path. There is only now.

All of us are doing the best we can with the information we have in the present moment. Our decisions, the paths we walk, are determined simply by moving forward instead of backward or staying in place. To live life is to make moment to moment decisions that decide the course of the path unfolding in front of us. Life doesn't offer you two choices like a toddler getting to pick between pizza and chicken tenders for dinner. There is only what we know now and what we decide to do with that knowledge.

You couldn't have done any differently. You're not bad,

deficient, inferior, or less worthy for walking the path that was in front of you.

Why are you sitting in judgment of yourself?

Maybe this is why we're so quick to judge each other—it's a welcome distraction from the unrelenting self-judgment we dish ourselves with each step we take down the path of now.

What would it look like to stop judging entirely? Yourself, and others?

What would it look like to just walk your path and accept what it holds, no matter how painful?

I'm not saying you should blindly stumble through life without thinking about the consequences of each step. Of course, be thoughtful. But that voice in your head that is *certain* that there were two doors, that at some point your path forked and you turned right when you should have turned left? That voice is a goddamned liar. That voice doesn't love you. That voice has one goal, and one goal only: make you suffer. Make you pay for this supposed "wrong choice."

It's not real.

And I guarantee you've already had enough judgment, anxiety, and regret to last a lifetime. So how about you put away the forever words and let Door #2 fade into the background?

It was never there at all.

IT IS AS IT IS

My friends *hate* when I pull them out of their would've, could've, should've realities.

I don't do it aggressively, or in an adversarial way. Totally the opposite, actually; I just let them talk.

They'll bring up a should've story and look at me, expecting me to say either "No, that's not true, don't beat yourself up," or, "You're goddamn right you should have; what the fuck did you expect to happen?" (The latter is actually just that liar voice in their head trying to find a villain to pin everything on.)

I say nothing. I just sit silently and stare at them. Occasionally, I'll say simply, "Tell me more."

Here's the thing about a long, drawn-out silence:

People can't stand it.

Some people truly crawl out of their skin in the face of silence. They *have* to fill the space.

Conveniently, they usually fill that space with more of their own made-up forever word stories, and after a few minutes, it clicks in their own ears how ridiculous they sound. They typically stop and glare at me.

"I mean, I guess I couldn't have changed it," they say, in a way that tells me that all they wanted was to be the villain so they'd have someone to blame.

I don't do that. We're not about self-blame at Her Well Wisher.

In my opinion, part of supporting someone is gently, lovingly, introducing them to the harsh reality they're actually living in, and pulling them out of their wells of forever words, their endless story landscapes where they're the villain and hero at the same time. It's okay to be honest with people about the reality they're in. In fact, sometimes it's the kindest thing you can do for them.

It is as it is, as Eckhart Tolle says.

The pain of living with what *is*, right now, is also the pain of loving what *was*.

You can certainly reflect in a healthy way. *If I'm ever presented with this situation again, I'm going to know that the path I took this time is an option, and it brought me to my present outcome. But I'm also going to know that a different path is also possible and might have a different outcome. I'm going to do whatever feels right in the moment.*

The thing I try to avoid is living in the future. *I have to make sure to avoid that. I can't ever let that happen again.* I'm going to go out on a limb and say your task list is already packed. Don't give yourself more to do. Every little "you better not do *that* again" instruction you give yourself is just another tick of anxiety on that never-ending task list.

Don't berate yourself for the past—but also don't set an impossible standard for the future.

Living right where you are, living now, does mean you have to open yourself to acceptance of the shit-kick life has dealt you. You can't escape to the past or future; you have to just let the kick come for your face, knock out a few teeth, and leave you reeling.

But *now* is also the only time the people who love you can actually be with you. They can't travel with you to the past and help push you to Door #2. They can't go with you to the future and point out the same kick coming for your face, help you duck out of the way and avoid it.

They can only be with you now. The past and present only exist inside your mind.

By opening yourself to the kick, you're also opening yourself to someone you love catching you, holding you up, and making sure you're okay.

There are things in life that truly knock us on our ass. Death. Divorce. Suicide. Cancer. And honestly, any number of other "lesser" tragedies that don't feel lesser at all, and shouldn't be diminished as "not tragic *enough*". You can drown in six feet of water, and you can also drown in six inches of water. It's all drowning.

The people we love will pull us out of the water if we let them.

So let them. Be here now.

Now holds all the pain, true. But it also holds all the love.

WHEN YOU HEAL FROM A **TRAGEDY**, THAT'S A **DIFFERENT** YOU. THE TRAGEDY DIDN'T MAKE THAT PERSON; THE **HEALING** DID.

CONCLUSION

One final well-intentioned word that I really, *really* recommend you don't fucking say:

"Everything you went through made you who you are."

Charlotte, I know I've been hard on you in this book, and you know it's because I love you. But that? That was some *bullshit*. Don't say that to anyone else.

Why the hell would I want to be defined by the worst moments in my life?

Are you suggesting that it's a good thing I went through those things, because it made me who I am?

Honestly, I could have done without it. I could have gotten tough without losing Jakob. I could have learned not to take shit from people without the drama and PTSD of Jax's birth. I could have become more empathetic without getting cancer. Those things may have sped up the process, but they didn't make me who I am.

And that's actually something I want to gently and lovingly make clear to all of you reading who are identifying more with me than with Charlotte:

Your tragedies don't make you who you are.

More than that, they don't make you *virtuous*. They don't make you a good person. They don't give you a pass.

I ran into a lot of fellow tragedy-sufferers during the various legs of my own personal bad-times marathon, and it didn't take long for me to pick out a certain type of person—the ones who were living as though the shit life had dealt them gave them a get out of jail free card on accountability. I watched them be crappy to nurses, to their spouses, to service workers. I watched them introduce themselves *as* their tragedy: "I'm a NICU mom" or "I'm a cancer fighter". Their entire identity was wrapped up in the roundhouse kick life had dealt them, and they clearly thought it meant they didn't have to keep being a good human at the same time.

Well, you know what? A lot of real shitheads have also gotten cancer. Or lost kids. They were shitty before it happened, they were shitty after it happened, and the fact that they went through tragedy didn't wipe away their bad behavior.

No matter what's going on in our lives, we all have a responsibility to continue to evolve into the best versions of ourselves we can be.

And if your life story revolves around the reasons why you can't, that's something to think about.

Lead with accountability. It's not my fault my son died. It's not my fault Cole committed suicide. It's not my fault I got cancer.

But it *is* my responsibility to navigate the aftermath as the person I want to be.

"All of those tragedies make you *you*."

No, fuck that. No. What makes me *me* is how I respond. How I heal.

There are a million different versions of you as you move through your life. When you heal from a tragedy, that's a different you. The tragedy didn't make that person; the healing did.

To live in reality and open yourself to everything it brings—all the pain, yes, but also all the love and support from the people who have your back—is to understand that it's not the tragedy that makes you.

It's the journey through healing afterward. That's where you evolve.

I did go through a whole lot of shit. Life really threw it at me there for a while—and I'm still getting some of the ripple effects on the daily. Thanks, life!

But what I went through isn't who I am.

I went through it and healed, and now I carry it like a backpack. I'm the same person. I just have a little weight on my shoulders now.

Luckily, I have people who love me, and their support keeps that weight feeling doable.

PEOPLE ARE AMAZING

In the aftermath of everything I've been through, and in the wake of all the well-intentioned words that have barraged me over the years, one thing has become clearer than ever:

People are amazing.

I can't even count how many times the loving allies in my life gave active support by just showing up on my doorstep and asking what was needed. From making meals for the boys, to hunting down specific soups I requested, to walking the dog, even just to leaving thoughtful notes and cards for me to read...it was all incredible. To those of you who brought over plants to brighten the space: that was so lovely. (But maybe don't do that. Sick people can barely take care of themselves, let alone houseplants, and the way they wither and die before our eyes evokes our own mortality to an unsettling degree.) The friendship of all these allies was the key to my healing through everything life dealt me, and I wouldn't be here if it weren't for these amazing people who showed up with nothing but love and support.

There were other people who taught me lessons along the way, too, and they were the people who left. See, when you go through tragedy, or when you get sick, you're in a different place. You're a bit of a different person, going through that. And sometimes there are people in your life who don't want to know the version of you carrying the backpack. They don't want to go along for the ride.

Initially, I felt angry, abandoned, incredulous that friends had just flat out abandoned me and my kid and my family. But today I realize I have nothing but gratitude. So, to all of you who left: *thank you*. You leaving made space for real connections and friendships, more space for the allies who have my back.

Who would have thought that the best classroom in the world for relationships is simply going through a hard time? I learned more about people in the past ten years than in the entire rest of my life combined.

I learned that it's okay to accept help.

I learned that it's okay to need it. It doesn't make you weak; it makes you human.

I learned that there's no rush to get through a tragedy. You're allowed to heal on your own schedule.

I learned that people *will* show up when you need them. And that you can count on people not to let you down.

I'm more optimistic than ever about people. I believe with

my whole heart that the vast majority of people out there truly want nothing more than to love and support the people in their lives.

And I hope this book helps you do that even better.

No more silver linings. No more would've, could've, should've. No more punches in the gut.

Build her up, wish her well...and *don't fucking say that!*

ACKN*WLEDGMENTS

Thank you to my kid, Jax. You have been stronger than a kid "should" have to be, and you always knew exactly what to say.

Brian, you are and always will be my compass.

Jakob, my forever blue heart, you were so beautiful. I've never loved so hard and so deep in such a quick moment.

To my favorite boy, Cole James: I miss you forever. Every breath is different without you, and I love you to the moon and back, infinity times. To those that have been destroyed by suicide, live for them and say their names! If it offends anyone, they can plug their ears and fuck off.

To my warrior sisters that I met on the way: thank you

for your strength and guidance, and for offering a space where I was allowed to be vulnerable without judgment. I will hold your love close forever.

To Janine Ott: we were diagnosed within weeks of each other, and you are missed. Brian still wears his pink bracelet in remembrance of you. I am so sorry cancer took you too early. Fuck you, cancer! And every woman reading this: please go get a mammogram! After I was diagnosed, I made it my mission to influence as many women as possible to self-check and get their mammograms. So far I'm up to 40 mammograms, 3 of which have led to a diagnosis. Get your mammograms!

To all the NICU moms and nurses: he's 11 now! What!? Thank you for making my crazy seem like normal everyday emotions. Remember, always wish her well first.

To Meghan McCracken and the entire team at Brilliant Media, thank you for taking a chance on this crazy idea. You helped translate my voice and words into exactly what I needed to say. It's been such an emotional rollercoaster; thank you for holding on and not jumping off. What a ride!

ABOUT THE AUTH*R

Mellissa Librach is an author, entrepreneur, and dedicated advocate for women's empowerment. As the founder of Her Well Wisher Fitness Studios, she combines her passion for physical wellness with emotional resilience, creating a supportive environment for women. Married to her best friend and a mother to two incredible souls, Mellissa's work, both in fitness and as an author, is driven by a commitment to realism and optimism, aiming to inspire and uplift others through shared experiences and genuine connections.

THE TOUGH TIMES GIFT G*VING GUIDE

Anytime someone we know goes through a hard time, the instinct is to get them something. However...sometimes it's hard to know what that "something" should be. With that in mind, here's a guide to all the *best* gifts I got during all my tough times, the ones that really did make my day better. (And I might have thrown in a few that I only *wish* I got. You're welcome.)

Time! Uninterrupted time, scheduled time, either one—just follow through with giving your time. Literally the best support possible.

Validation! It's a gift to be seen in action, validated and heard!

Body products (my favorite are from Dirty Lamb).

Glass water bottle. When you get chemotherapy everything tastes like metal except plastic and glass, and hydration is essential.

Beanies and comfy blankets ever. The company Love Your Melon donates to pediatric cancer!

Soups (made to their specific likes—just ask them exactly what they can and can't eat). I had a freezer full of soup.

Favorite restaurant gift cards, local grocery store gift card, coffeeshop gift cards.

Thank-you cards. I wanted to send thank-yous to people and I bought myself stationary to sent thanks for all that so many did for me. A friend said to me, "Oh, that's a good gift for next time!" My response: "There will *not* be a next time..."

Pedicure to their favorite place with extra massage!

Body heating pad and blanket for after treatments to each the aches.

Playdates for the kid(s).

Playlists! I like coloring and watching TV but during treatment it was a challenge sometimes to focus or keep my eyes open, so music was healing.

Sweatsuits with a soft zip front. I was gifted an Aviator Nation sweatsuit and it ruined me for all others!

Strong AF bracelet from the Little Words Project.

Front button super comfy PJs.

Pillow.

Kitchen towels and bathroom towels. Cancer patients and Preemie moms have to wash their hand towels every day to prevent the spread of viruses. Same with sheets! (All cotton-it helps with hot flashes.)

Mastectomy belt (google it), 2 or 3 of these are important for showering!

Silk pillow cases to help with hair loss and skin irritation. Get multiple, because these have to be washed frequently.

Socks! my favorite pictures in Chemo included socks with "BRAVE" and "STRONG" on the soles.

ANYONE COULD BE STRUGGLING WITH SUICIDE.

THE 988 LIFELINE PROVIDES 24/7, FREE AND CONFIDENTIAL SUPPORT FOR PEOPLE IN DISTRESS, PREVENTION AND CRISIS RESOURCES FOR YOU OR YOUR LOVED ONES.

JUST DIAL 988.

Made in the USA
Columbia, SC
05 August 2024

39402126R00131